# AMERICAN
# COOKING FOR
# FOREIGN LANDS

# AMERICAN COOKING FOR FOREIGN LANDS

Maj-Greth Wegener

**NORTH CASTLE BOOKS**
Greenwich, Connecticut 06830
U.S.A.

# CONTENTS

## CHAPTER SIX • MISCELLANEOUS 161

## INDEX 173

## APPENDIX 180

# MEASUREMENTS

The recipes in this book are given in American measurements, mostly spoons and 8-ounce cups; and in metric measurements, chiefly spoons, deciliters and grams. The tablespoon, holding $\frac{1}{2}$ fluid ounce, and the teaspoon of $\frac{1}{6}$ ounce are not official measurements, but are used internationally in cooking and have about the same capacity everywhere except in British imperial areas.

Metric amounts have often been approximated to avoid inconvenient fractions. There are tables of measurement, weight and temperature in the Appendix for those who are interested in knowing the exact equivalents.

If you are using a British imperial cup, which holds 10 fluid ounces, take $\frac{3}{4}$ of the cup measurements in these recipes. The official British tablespoon holds one ounce, and equals two American tablespoons. There is also an unofficial British tablespoon which holds $\frac{2}{3}$ of an ounce, or $1\frac{1}{3}$ American tablespoons. The British teaspoon holds either $\frac{1}{4}$ or $\frac{1}{6}$ ounce, while an American teaspoon holds $\frac{1}{6}$ ounce. If you have the unofficial size spoons, the error in using American measurements directly will be quite small.

## ABBREVIATIONS

| | | | |
|---|---|---|---|
| tbsp | tablespoon | dl | deciliter |
| tsp | teaspoon | l | liter |
| lb | pound | g | gram |
| " | inch | hg | hectogram |
| F | Fahrenheit | kg | kilogram |
| C | Celsius (Centigrade) | cm | centimeter |

# INTRODUCTION

This book consists of over 240 recipes that are representative of the best American cooking. They have been chosen for attractiveness and suitability to other countries. Both American and metric measurements are given for each item, for convenience in international use.

In the United States we are fortunate in having dozens of cook books bringing us recipes from all over the world, but this may be the first time that an American book has been prepared especially to take our ways of cooking to other countries. I hope that it will bring them at least a fraction of the pleasure that their cooking has brought to us.

I believe that the quality of American cooking is underestimated almost everywhere. There seems to be an international belief that American families eat directly out of cans and freezer packages, and have lost or not developed a representative and attractive cuisine. This is far from the truth, as it considers only the few homes where people do rely far too heavily on the TV dinner and other ready made work savers. In all countries there are some housewives who are not interested in cooking, and some people who don't care what they eat, and they should not be the standard for judging their country's culinary skill.

The average American housewife is a good cook, and she is often an excellent one. Her work in the kitchen has been made easier by the help of many kinds of household appliances, and she has an advantage in the availability of a large variety of both raw materials and processed foods. On the other hand, duties outside of the kitchen make big demands on her time.

1

The greater part of the population of the United States consists of the descendants of emigrants, the majority from Europe, but some from almost every country of the world. Their varied food cultures have acted upon each other, and have been affected by the differences in native foods on the new continent, and by the growth of new taste preferences.

These factors have combined to bring forth a cuisine which is different from any other, and which includes many very special dishes.

Many of the most popular American dishes are clearly foreign in origin, but some of them have been changed so much that they are often not readily recognized in their homelands. Examples are meat balls from Sweden, pizza from Italy, chili con carne from Mexico and chop suey from China. All of these are included, along with way-back American foods such as roast turkey, baked beans, jellied salads and apple pie.

The recipes in this book have been chosen from among thousands generally used in the United States. Each of them has been carefully tested in my kitchen, using both the American and the metric measurements of ingredients, whenever there was a difference between them. They have also been selected according to the availability of their ingredients throughout the world, and on the basis of probable acceptability to European and Latin palates. I have eliminated recipes that duplicate foods already known in most of the world, and those that are long and complicated, or whose mixing depends on appliances.

My appreciation and thanks go to all those who have given me advice and help in the preparation of this book. I am especially grateful to Mrs. Ingrid Lundén, teacher at the College for Home Economics in Gothenburg, who willingly, happily and with great patience assisted me in the preparation of the original Swedish edition.

I now hope that this book will give its readers just as much interest—and good eating—as I have enjoyed in its preparation.

Maj-Greth Wegener

# BAKING

A lot of baking is done in American homes, but it is seldom on the lavish scale common in northern Europe, where yeast breads, cakes and cookies are often served at the same time. The old custom of having seven kinds of cakes and cookies for the coffee or tea table has died out, and one or two varieties at a time are considered to be sufficient. Whether this cutting down is the result of out-of-kitchen interests, weight-watching or just a slight laziness is a question. In any case, it simplifies both the cooking and serving of goodies, but puts extra pressure on the hostess to make sure that the item she does serve should be very good.

Bread is generally served with meals here. Plain bread usually comes from the store, but specialties are most often baked at home. These include loaves using corn meal, oat meal and other special flours; and particularly little breads—soft rolls, muffins and biscuits of many kinds, most of which should be served hot or warm, with plenty of butter.

The most popular cakes are those that are covered with frosting, but the plain or almost-plain cakes baked in loaves or rings are common. Frosting makes a very sweet cake, particularly if there are two layers. I have several recipes for each type, so the choice among them is free. The angel cake is very special—other countries make it, but apparently not as often or in just the same way.

Cookies are good, but usually very simple. The drop cookie does not need rolling and seldom gets much decoration but the family sees to it that it disappears just as quickly as the cut-and-decorated beauties in other lands.

I have included pie crust among the baked goods, although

the pies themselves appear later among the desserts. This is not entirely satisfactory, particularly since pies are eaten almost as often as snacks with coffee or tea as for dessert, but it is the best arrangement I could work out.

Readers will notice that quantities have been adjusted between the American and metric measurements to avoid small fractions. This sometimes results in a difference in the recipe, and therefore in the baked product, when one column of quantities is used instead of the other. However, tests have been made both ways, and results from either column are within the normal variations expected in these foods.

Top: Angel Food Cake with whipped cream and shredded coconut, and Black Devils' Food cake with chocolate frosting.
Bottom: Sour Cream Cake, Silver Layer Cake with Vanilla frosting

# BISCUITS

*Biscuits are a very popular type of bread in the United States. They should be served directly out of the oven, piping hot with butter, or butter and jam, for breakfast or lunch. They can also be used for dinner with various main dishes, and are then served instead of either potatoes or bread.*

| | | |
|---|---|---|
| 2 cups | (5 dl) | flour |
| 4 tsp | (4 tsp) | baking powder |
| 1 tsp | (1 tsp) | salt |
| ¼ cup | (½ dl) | shortening (preferably vegetable shortening such as Spry or Crisco. Butter or margarine (60 g) can be used). |
| ¾ cup | (1¾ dl) | milk |

Sift together flour, baking powder and salt into a bowl. Add shortening and cut finely with two knives or a pastry blender until mixture is crumbly. Add milk and mix quickly to make a soft dough. Put on floured board and knead about 30 seconds, or until dough sticks together in a ball. Roll out or pat out dough until about ½" (or 1½ cm) thick. Cut out buns with round cooky cutter or a glass. Place them close together on an ungreased baking sheet and bake in a very hot oven—450° F or 230° C—10–12 minutes, or until they are golden brown. Serve immediately, piping hot, with butter or marmalade, jam or honey.

## Variations:

BACON BISCUITS
Proceed in the same way as above but add ⅓ cup (1 dl) drained, well-cooked bacon, broken into small bits.

CHIVES BISCUITS
Proceed in the same way as above, but add ¼ cup (½ dl) minced chives.

BUTTERMILK BISCUITS
In place of milk in the above recipe use buttermilk, but use only 2 tsp. baking powder and add ½ tsp. baking soda.

CHEESE BISCUITS
Proceed in the same way as above, but add a scant ½ cup (1 dl) grated cheese to the flour.

# STIR AND ROLL BISCUITS

| | | |
|---|---|---|
| 2 cups | (5 dl) | flour |
| 3 tsp | (3 tsp) | baking powder |
| 1 tsp | (1 tsp) | salt |
| ⅓ cup | (¾ dl) | salad oil |
| ⅔ cup | (1½ dl) | milk |

Sift together flour, baking powder and salt into a bowl. Pour in salad oil and milk all at once, and stir until mixture holds together and forms a ball. Put this on floured board and knead about 20 seconds, then roll or pat the dough until it is approximately ½″ thick. Cut with a round cutter, or a glass, and put these buns on an ungreased baking sheet. Bake 10–12 minutes in a very hot oven—475° F or 240° C. Serve biscuits piping hot with butter, jam, marmalade or honey. Variations of these can be made in the same manner as for preceding recipe for biscuits.

# OATMEAL MUFFINS

| | | |
|---|---|---|
| 1 cup | (2½ dl) | oatmeal |
| 1 cup | (2½ dl) | buttermilk or sour milk |
| 1 | (1) | egg |
| ⅔ cup | (1½ dl) | brown sugar |
| 1 cup | (2½ dl) | flour |
| 1 tsp | (1 tsp) | salt |
| 1 tsp | (1 tsp) | baking powder |
| ½ tsp | (½ tsp) | baking soda |
| ½ cup | (1 dl) | melted butter or margarine |

Soak oatmeal in buttermilk or sour milk for one hour, add egg and beat well. Mix in sugar, then in flour sifted with salt, baking powder and soda. Add cooled melted butter. Bake in greased muffin pans in hot oven—400° F or 210° C—15–20 minutes. Makes 10–12 muffins.

# CORN BREAD

*I am including this recipe although I know that at the present time real corn meal can be obtained only in specialty stores in some parts of the world. But corn bread is so typically American that it demands a place in this book, even if it cannot be made everywhere.*

| | | |
|---|---|---|
| 1 | (1) | **egg** |
| 1 cup | (2½ dl) | **milk** |
| ¼ cup | (½ dl) | **flour, sifted** |
| 1¼ cups | (3 dl) | **corn meal** |
| 3 tbsp | (3 tbsp) | **sugar** |
| 3 tsp | (3 tsp) | **baking powder** |
| 1 tsp | (1 tsp) | **salt** |
| 3 tbsp | (3 tbsp) | **shortening, preferably vegetable shortening such as Spry or Crisco. Butter or margarine can also be used.** |

Beat together egg and milk and blend with remaining ingredients, which first have been mixed together. Pour into a greased, square baking pan or muffin pan. Bake in a very hot oven—450° F or 230° C—10–15 minutes for muffins, or 10–25 minutes if in a baking pan. Serve piping hot with butter.

# ANADAMA BREAD

*There is a story to explain the name of this bread. The first loaf is supposed to have been made by a fisherman in Massachusetts who had a lazy wife named Anna. Each day he looked jealously at his fellow fishermen when they opened their lunch boxes and took out home-baked bread and other goodies while he found just cold corn meal mush in his.*

*One morning he lost his temper while watching her mix up a batch of mush. He pushed her out of the kitchen, stirred some yeast and flour into the mush and put the mixture into the oven, while muttering "Anna, damn her, Anna-dama, Annadama—". The bread that resulted was stuck with the name he gave it.*

*You may not wish to believe this story, but have you a better explanation for its name? Anyhow, it is a very good bread, and if you can't get real corn meal you can substitute cream of wheat.*

| | | |
|---|---|---|
| 1½ cups | (4 dl) | water |
| 1 tbsp | (1 tbsp) | salt |
| ⅓ cup | (1 dl) | corn meal (or in lack of this, cream of wheat) |
| ⅓ cup | (1 dl) | molasses |
| 1½ tbsp | (1½ tbsp) | shortening |
| 1 tbsp | (1 tbsp) | dry yeast *or* |
| 1 | (25 g) | yeast cake |
| ¼ cup | (½ dl) | lukewarm water with 1 tsp sugar |
| About 1 lb | (½ kg) | flour |
| (4–5 cups) | (1 l) | |

Bring water to boil in a saucepan, then add salt and cornmeal, stirring constantly. Pour into large mixing bowl and add molasses and shortening. Let mixture cool until lukewarm. Add yeast, dissolved in water with sugar, and half of the flour and mix well. Add sufficient flour to make an easily handled dough, which is placed on floured board and kneaded until elastic. Let the dough rise until double in bulk, knead again for a while and put in a greased bread pan. Let rise until almost double in bulk, about one hour, and bake in a moderate oven—375° F or 190° C—40–50 minutes. This recipe makes one large loaf, but it can be easily doubled or made into three loaves by increasing the ingredients proportionally.

# OATMEAL BREAD

*A delicious, moist bread with real oat flavor.*

| | | |
|---|---|---|
| 2 cups | (5 dl) | quick-cooking oatmeal |
| ½ cup | (1¼ dl) | molasses |
| ½ cup | (110 g) | butter or margarine |
| 1½ tbsp | (1½ tbsp) | salt |
| ½ cup | (1¼ dl) | sugar |
| 3 cups | (8 dl) | boiling water |
| 2 tbsp | (2 tbsp) | dry yeast *or* |
| 2 | (50 g) | yeast cakes |
| ⅓ cup | (1 dl) | lukewarm water |
| About 4½ lbs | (2 kg) | flour |
| (16–18 cups) | (4 l) | |

Mix oatmeal, molasses, shortening, salt and sugar in a large mixing bowl. Pour on the boiling water and let the mixture cool until lukewarm. Dissolve yeast in ⅓ cup (1 dl) lukewarm water with a pinch of sugar and pour into oatmeal mixture. Add about 2 cups (5 dl) flour and mix and then sufficient additional flour to make a firm dough, which does not stick to hands. Place dough on floured board and knead until smooth and elastic. Cover with a clean towel and let rise in a warm place about 2 hours. Knead dough again, cut up into six parts and make loaves of these. Let rise for one more hour and bake in medium hot oven—400° F or 200° C—40–50 minutes.

Anadama Bread

# ENGLISH MUFFINS

*English muffins are not at all like any other muffins. They are small, thin, flat, rather tough cakes, made with a yeast dough and "baked" on a griddle or a frying pan on top of the stove. They are always used toasted, and should be served hot with butter and jam.*

| | | |
|---|---|---|
| 1 tbsp | (1 tbsp) | dry yeast *or* |
| 1 | (25 g) | yeast cake |
| 2 tbsp | (2 tbsp) | sugar |
| ½ cup | (1 dl) | lukewarm water |
| 1¼ cups | (3 dl) | lukewarm milk |
| 4 tbsp | (4 tbsp) | melted butter or margarine |
| 2 tsp | (2 tsp) | salt |
| About 1 lb | (½ kg) | flour |
| (4–5 cups) | (1 l) | |

Dissolve yeast in sugar and lukewarm water. Heat milk till lukewarm, add butter, salt, a little of the flour and yeast mixture, then add remaining flour. Knead dough on lightly floured board until smooth and elastic. Place dough in greased bowl, cover and let rise in a warm place until double in bulk. Roll out dough ¾–1″ (2–3 cm) thick and cut round cakes with a cutter or a large glass (about 3″ or 10 cm in diameter) and let them rise. Heat a griddle or a large, greased frying pan, until fairly hot and place cakes on it and bake, turning frequently, until muffins are done, about 15 minutes. The muffins can also be baked in a moderate oven—400° F or 210° C—10–15 minutes. The cakes should be turned over after half the baking time so an "undercrust" will be formed on both sides. Serve split in half with butter or marmalade. These split muffins can also be used for pizza pie in which case the pizza filling is placed on the broken or cut surface.

# SPOON BREAD

*Spoon bread is something in between bread and pudding, and is served as a side dish with meat and gravy. It is made mostly in the South, where it is often served instead of potatoes. Cream of wheat can be substituted for corn meal if necessary.*

Spoon Bread

| 1 cup | (2½ dl) | corn meal (or lacking this, cream of wheat) |
| 1 tsp | (1 tsp) | salt |
| 1 cup | (2½ dl) | milk |
| 2 tbsp | (2 tbsp) | butter or margarine |
| 3 | (3) | eggs |
| 1 tsp | (1 tsp) | baking powder |

Bring 2 cups of water (5 dl) to a boil in a medium saucepan and stir in corn meal, a little at a time, together with the salt, stirring constantly and letting mixture cook on very low heat until thickened. Remove from heat, add milk and butter and beat vigorously. Place saucepan in cold water so that mixture cools. Beat egg whites until stiff, and then beat egg yolks until thick and light. Add the yolks together with the baking powder to the corn meal mixture in saucepan and stir well. Carefully fold in egg whites and mix lightly. Then pour into a greased baking dish and bake without cover in medium hot oven—375° F or 190° C—40-50 minutes or until the "bread" is golden brown in color and of very fluffy consistency.

# RAISIN APPLE COFFEE CAKE

*This recipe is popular, as it is easy and quick to make and practically never fails. It appears in some European cook books and women's magazines, in more or less the same form as "American Coffee Cake."*

| | | |
|---|---|---|
| ¾ cup | (1¾ dl) | sugar |
| 3 tbsp | (3 tbsp) | butter or margarine |
| 1 | (1) | egg |
| ½ cup | (1¼ dl) | milk |
| 1½ cups | (4 dl) | flour |
| 2½ tsp | (2½ tsp) | baking powder |
| ½ tsp | (½ tsp) | salt |
| ½ cup | (1 dl) | raisins |
| | | apple slices |

Mix sugar, butter or margarine and egg thoroughly, stir in milk. Sift together flour, baking powder and salt and stir in. Add raisins and spread batter in greased and floured baking pan. Arrange thinly sliced apples in nice design on top of batter, and sprinkle top with 1 tsp. cinnamon mixed with 1 tbsp. sugar. Bake in medium oven–375° F or 190° C–25–35 minutes, until wooden toothpick thrust into center comes out clean. Can be served either warm or cold.

# COWBOY COFFEE CAKE

| | | |
|---|---|---|
| 1¼ cups | (3 dl) | flour |
| 1 cup | (2½ dl) | brown sugar |
| ½ tsp | (½ tsp) | salt |
| ⅓ cup | (80 g) | butter or margarine |
| 1½ tsp | (1½ tsp) | baking powder |
| ¼ tsp | (¼ tsp) | baking soda |
| ½ tsp | (½ tsp) | cinnamon |
| ¼ tsp | (¼ tsp) | nutmeg |
| ½ cup | (1¼ dl) | sour milk |
| 1 | (1) | well-beaten egg |

Combine flour, brown sugar, salt and butter or margarine in a large bowl and mix until crumbly. Reserve ½ cup (1 dl) of this mixture to sprinkle on top of cake. To remaining crumbs, add baking powder, baking soda and spices and mix thoroughly. Add milk and egg and stir until smooth. Pour into greased baking pan, sprinkle with reserved crumbs, and if desired a little more cinnamon. Bake in moderately hot oven—375° F or 190° C—25-30 minutes. This cake tastes best if served warm.

## SOUR CREAM CAKE

*This cake holds its moisture very well, so that it keeps fresh for a long time.*

| | | |
|---|---|---|
| ½ cup | (110 g) | butter or margarine |
| 1 cup | (2½ dl) | sugar |
| 2 cups | (5 dl) | flour |
| 1½ tsp | (1½ tsp) | baking soda |
| 1 tsp | (1 tsp) | baking powder |
| ½ tsp | (½ tsp) | salt |
| 2 | (2) | eggs |
| 1 cup | (2½ dl) | sour cream |
| 1 tsp | | vanilla extract *or* |
| | (1 tbsp) | vanilla sugar |
| 2 tbsp | (2 tbsp) | milk |
| 1 tsp | (1 tsp) | cinnamon, mixed with |
| ¼ cup | (½ dl) | sugar |

Cream butter and sugar, add eggs, and beat. Add sour cream and milk, mixing well. Sift together flour, baking soda, baking powder and salt and add to batter, a little at a time. Add vanilla. Pour half of batter in a greased ring pan, which should be rather large, and sprinkle on half of cinnamon and sugar mixture. Pour in the rest of the batter and sprinkle with remaining cinnamon and sugar. Bake in medium oven—350° F or 175° C—35-40 minutes. Let the cake cool about 10-15 minutes before it is taken out of pan.

Slivered almonds may be sprinkled on top before baking, if desired.

# SPECKLE CAKE

*There are parts of the world where it is difficult to find unsweetened chocolate. Dark, semisweet chocolate may be used instead, with excellent results.*

| | | |
|---|---|---|
| 1 cup | (2½ dl) | sugar |
| ½ cup | (110 g) | butter or margarine |
| 2 cups | (5 dl) | flour |
| 3½ tsp | (3½ tsp) | baking powder |
| ½ tsp | (½ tsp) | salt |
| 1½ tsp | | vanilla extract *or* |
| | (1 tbsp) | vanilla sugar |
| 1 cup | (2½ dl) | milk |
| 3 | (3) | egg whites beaten with ½ cup (1 dl) sugar |
| 2 oz | (50 g) | unsweetened chocolate, grated roughly |

Cream butter and add sugar gradually. Add flour, mixed with salt and baking powder, alternately with the milk. Add grated chocolate and vanilla and fold in stiffly beaten egg whites. Bake cake in moderate oven—300–325° F or 150–160° C—for 45 minutes. The cake can be used plain or covered with frosting.

Sour Cream Cake

## CHEF'S SPICED CAKE

| | | |
|---|---|---|
| 2 cups | (5 dl) | sugar |
| 2 cups | (5 dl) | cold coffee—not too strong |
| ½ cup | (1¼ dl) | shortening |
| | | pinch of salt |
| ¾ cup | (2 dl) | raisins |
| 3 cups | (7½ dl) | flour |
| 2½ tsp | (2½ tsp) | baking soda |
| 1 tsp | (1 tsp) | cinnamon |
| 1 tsp | (1 tsp) | ginger |
| 1 tsp | (1 tsp) | ground cloves |

Pour sugar, coffee, shortening and salt in a heavy saucepan and let it boil for a few minutes. Cool slightly and add flour, mixed with baking soda and spices. Mix the batter well and pour into a rather large ring pan and bake in medium oven—350° F or 175° C—about one hour.

## QUICK GINGERBREAD CAKE

| | | |
|---|---|---|
| 1 | (1) | egg |
| ½ cup | (1¼ dl) | sugar |
| ½ cup | (1¼ dl) | salad oil (or melted butter or margarine) |
| ½ cup | (1¼ dl) | molasses |
| 2 cups | (5 dl) | flour |
| ½ tsp | (½ tsp) | baking powder |
| 1 tsp | (1 tsp) | baking soda |
| 2 tsp | (2 tsp) | ginger |
| 1 tsp | (1 tsp) | cinnamon |
| ½ tsp | (½ tsp) | ground cloves |
| ⅔ cup | (1½ dl) | boiling water |

In a bowl, beat the egg, add sugar, salad oil and molasses and mix thoroughly. Sift together flour, baking powder, baking soda, salt and spices and add to the first mixture alternately with the boiling water. Pour into a greased pan and bake in a moderate oven—350° F or 175° C—for about 40 minutes. This cake is good to serve warm with apple sauce and whipped cream, and can, of course, also be served cold.

## EASY OATMEAL CAKE

| | | |
|---|---|---|
| 1 cup | (2½ dl) | oatmeal |
| ½ cup | (1¼ dl) | boiling water |
| ½ cup | (110 g) | butter or margarine |
| 2 cups | (5 dl) | brown sugar |
| 1 cup | (2½ dl) | sugar (white) |
| 2 | (2) | eggs |
| 1 tsp | (1 tsp) | cinnamon |
| 1½ tsp | (1½ tsp) | baking soda |
| 1½ cups | (4 dl) | flour |
| ½ cup | (1¼ dl) | milk |
| 1 cup | (3 dl—125 g) | shredded coconut |
| 1 scant cup | (2 dl) | chopped pecans (or other nuts) |

Combine oatmeal, boiling water and butter. Beat 1 cup brown sugar (2½ dl), white sugar and eggs and add to oatmeal mixture. Add cinnamon and flour, mixed with baking soda, and mix well. Pour into large greased and floured baking pan, about 9 x 13″ (20 x 30 cm). Bake in medium oven—350° F or 175° C—approximately 30 minutes. Mix together milk, coconut, nuts and remaining 1 cup (2½ dl) brown sugar and spread over cake, put pan under broiler until the top is brown. This is a rather big cake but it can be made half-size by cutting all the ingredients in half.

## STREUSEL-FILLED CAKE

| | | |
|---|---|---|
| ¾ cup | (1¾ dl) | sugar |
| 3 tbsp | (3 tbsp) | butter or margarine |
| 1 | (1) | egg |
| ½ cup | (1¼ dl) | milk |
| 1½ cups | (4 dl) | flour |
| 2½ tsp | (2½ tsp) | baking powder |
| ½ tsp | (½ tsp) | salt |

**Streusel Mixture:**

| | | |
|---|---|---|
| ½ cup | (1¼ dl) | sugar |
| 2 tbsp | (2 tbsp) | flour |
| 2 tsp | (2 tsp) | cinnamon |
| 2 tbsp | (2 tbsp) | melted butter |
| ½ cup | (1 dl) | chopped nuts |

Cream butter, sugar and egg, add milk. Mix together the dry ingredients, sift them and add to batter. Spread half of batter in greased and floured baking pan, sprinkle half of streusel mixture on this (all ingredients of topping should first be well mixed), then spread remaining batter and on top remaining streusel mixture. Bake in medium warm oven—350° F or 175° C—25–35 minutes. Test with a toothpick in center of cake to make sure it is done.

## MAGIC TOPPING CAKE

| | | |
|---|---|---|
| 1 cup | (2½ dl) | flour |
| 1½ tsp | (1½ tsp) | baking powder |
| ¼ tsp | (¼ tsp) | salt |
| 1 cup | (2½ dl) | sugar |
| 2 | (2) | eggs |
| 1 tsp | | vanilla extract *or* |
| | (2 tsp) | vanilla sugar |
| 2 tbsp | (2 tbsp) | butter or margarine |
| ½ cup, scant | (1 dl) | milk |

**Topping:**

| | | |
|---|---|---|
| 1 cup, scant | (2 dl) | shredded coconut |
| 1 cup, scant | (2 dl) | brown sugar |
| ½ tsp | (½ tsp) | salt |
| 6 tbsp | (6 tbsp) | butter or margarine |
| 2 tbsp | (2 tbsp) | milk |

Beat eggs until thick and foamy, gradually add sugar. The longer you beat this, the better the cake will be. Heat milk and butter until hot, but mixture must not boil. Sift flour together with salt and baking powder and add to egg mixture, then add the hot milk and stir batter only until mixture is smooth. Pour batter in greased and floured baking pan and bake in medium oven—350° F or 175° C—about 30 minutes. In the meantime mix all ingredients for topping in a heavy saucepan and cook until blended and melted, stirring constantly. Spread on top of warm cake and broil 2″ from heat, watching constantly, or it will burn. (It is very important to spread topping on cake while it is still hot, otherwise it will separate from it).

## ORANGE MARMALADE CAKE

| | | |
|---|---|---|
| 1¾ cups | (4½ dl) | flour |
| 2 tsp | (2 tsp) | baking powder |
| ½ tsp | (½ tsp) | salt |
| ¼ cup | (½ dl) | sugar |
| ½ cup, scant | (1 dl) | chopped walnuts (or almonds) |
| 2 | (2) | eggs |
| ½ cup | (1¼ dl) | milk |
| 2 tbsp | (2 tbsp) | melted butter |
| ½ cup, scant | (1 dl) | orange marmalade |

Sift together flour, baking powder and salt. Add sugar and nuts. Cream eggs, milk and melted butter and add to flour mixture. Stir in orange marmalade and mix well. Bake in moderate oven in loaf pan—350° F or 175° C—50-60 minutes. Remove from pan and spread with orange marmalade while cake is still warm. The top may also be decorated with walnut halves or chopped almonds.

## RHUBARB CAKE

| | | |
|---|---|---|
| 1 cup | (2½ dl) | sour cream |
| 1 tsp | (1 tsp) | baking soda |
| 1 cup | (2½ dl) | sugar |
| 2 cups | (5 dl) | flour |
| 1 tsp | (1 tsp) | nutmeg |
| 2 cups | (5 dl) | rhubarb, finely cut |

In a bowl, mix together sour cream and baking soda. Add sugar and beat. Sift flour with nutmeg and stir into cream mixture. Fold the rhubarb into it carefully. Bake in greased, floured baking dish in medium oven—350° F or 175° C—about 40 minutes until the cake is a golden brown. Serve as a dessert with whipped cream or vanilla sauce, or plain with coffee or tea.

## PINEAPPLE COCONUT CAKE

| | | |
|---|---|---|
| ½ cup | (110 g) | butter or margarine |
| ¾ cup | (2 dl) | sugar |
| 2 | (2) | eggs |
| 2 cups | (5 dl) | flour |
| 1½ tsp | (1½ tsp) | baking powder |
| ½ tsp | (½ tsp) | baking soda |
| ¼ tsp | (¼ tsp) | salt |
| | | pinch of ginger |
| ⅔ cup | (1½ dl) | crushed pineapple |

**Topping:**

| | | |
|---|---|---|
| 1 cup | (2½ dl) | shredded coconut |
| ½ cup | (1¼ dl) | crushed pineapple |

Cream sugar with butter or margarine until thick, add eggs and beat until mixture thickens further. Sift together flour, baking powder, baking soda, salt and ginger and add these ingredients to batter alternately with ⅔ cup (1½ dl) crushed pineapple. When batter is well mixed, pour into a greased and floured baking pan. In a small bowl, mix together remaining ½ cup (1¼ dl) pineapple

Black and White Striped Cake, Pineapple Coconut Cake, Black Devils' Food Cake

and coconut and spread this mixture evenly on batter. Bake in medium-warm oven—375° F or 190° C—30-35 minutes. Test with a toothpick to see if cake is ready. Let it cool, then cut it up and serve directly out of the pan.

## COCONUT MERINGUE CAKE

| | | |
|---|---|---|
| ½ cup plus 2 tbsp | (125 g) | butter or margarine |
| ⅔ cup | (1½ dl) | sugar |
| 3 | (3) | egg yolks |
| 1 cup | (2½ dl) | flour |
| 2 tsp | (2 tsp) | baking powder |

Cream sugar and butter or margarine. Beat egg yolks until light and lemon colored and add to butter mixture. Stir in flour, mixed and sifted with baking powder. Pour batter in a greased and floured baking pan. On top of this, spread a meringue made as follows:

| | | |
|---|---|---|
| 3 | (3) | egg whites |
| ⅔ cup | (1½ dl) | sugar |
| 1⅔ cups | (4 dl, about 125 g) | shredded coconut |

Beat egg whites until stiff, add sugar a little at a time and continue beating until all sugar is melted and meringue is thick and glossy. Carefully fold in coconut.

Bake cake in medium oven—350° F or 175° C—about 40 minutes.

## BLITZ TORTE

| | | |
|---|---|---|
| 4 | (4) | eggs |
| 1½ cups | (4 dl) | sugar |
| 1 cup | (2½ dl) | flour |
| 1 tsp | (1 tsp) | baking powder |
| 5 tbsp | (5 tbsp) | butter or margarine |
| 3 tbsp | (3 tbsp) | milk |

Top: Sour Cream Cake, page 13

Bottom: Strawberry Shortcake, page 28

**Decoration:**

| ½ cup | (1 dl) | shredded coconut |
|-------|--------|------------------|
| ½ cup | (1 dl) | chopped almonds or other nuts |
| ½–1 cup | (1–2 dl) | whipping cream |

Cream together butter and ⅓ of the sugar until fluffy. Add egg yolks, then milk and flour and mix well. Place batter, which is rather thick, in two greased and floured baking pans of exactly the same size (half in each), flour your hand and flatten the batter with it. Beat egg whites until stiff, gradually add remaining sugar and continue beating until thick and glossy. Spread half of meringue on top of batter in each cake pan, sprinkle with coconut and chopped almonds or nuts and bake in medium oven—350° F or 175° C—25-30 minutes. When the cakes have cooled, one is put on top of the other with whipped cream in between and served immediately thereafter.

## ORANGE COCONUT CREAM ROLL

| 3 | (3) | eggs |
|---|-----|------|
| 1 cup | (2½ dl) | sugar |
| ½ cup, scant | (1 dl) | fresh orange juice |
| 1 cup | (2½ dl) | flour |
| 2 tsp | (2 tsp) | baking powder |
| | | pinch of salt |
| 1 cup | (2½ dl—about 75 g) | shredded coconut |
| 1 cup | (2 dl) | heavy cream, whipped |

In a bowl beat eggs until light and lemon-colored. Gradually beat in sugar, add orange juice alternately with the flour, sifted together with baking powder and salt. Spread in shallow pan on an oiled brown paper—about 10 x 15″ (25 x 40 cm). Bake in medium-hot oven—375° F or 190° C—10-12 minutes. Test with a toothpick. If ready, turn immediately onto fresh paper, sprinkled with a little confectioners' sugar. Carefully remove paper from cake, trim edges which might have become dry and hard during baking and roll like a jelly roll. Cool on rack. To serve, unroll it, spread with whipped cream and coconut, re-roll and let it stand in refrigerator a short while before serving.

Tuna Loaf, page 50

# ORANGE NUT LOAF

*Loaf cakes, which are baked in bread pans, are typically American. They can be eaten plain, with butter or with sauce.*

| | | |
|---|---|---|
| ¾ cup | (1¾ dl) | sugar |
| 2 tbsp | (2 tbsp) | butter or margarine |
| 1 | (1) | egg |
| ¾ cup | (1¾ dl) | milk |
| ¾ cup | (1¾ dl) | orange juice (freshly pressed, about 2 oranges) |
| 2 tbsp | (2 tbsp) | grated orange rind |
| 3 cups | (8 dl) | flour |
| 4 tsp | (4 tsp) | baking powder |
| 1 tsp | (1 tsp) | salt |
| ½ cup | (1 dl) | chopped nuts or almonds |

In a bowl mix thoroughly sugar, butter and egg, add milk, orange juice and the grated orange rind. Sift together flour and baking powder and add to batter, then add chopped nuts. Pour batter in a greased, floured loaf pan, about 5 x 9″ (10 x 20 cm), and let stand for about 20 minutes before baking. Bake about 70 minutes in medium oven—350° F or 175° C. A crack in the top is characteristic for this cake.

# APRICOT LOAF

| | | |
|---|---|---|
| ½ cup | (1 dl) | dried apricots, cut up into bits and soaked in water for ½ hour |
| 1 | (1) | egg |
| 1 cup | (2½ dl) | sugar |
| 2 tbsp | (2 tbsp) | butter |
| 1¾ cups | (4½ dl) | flour |
| 3 tsp | (3 tsp) | baking powder |
| 1 tsp | (1 tsp) | baking soda |
| 1 tsp | (1 tsp) | salt |
| ⅔ cup | (1½ dl) | orange juice |
| | | chopped nuts or almonds, if desired |

Cream butter and sugar, add egg and stir until smooth and fluffy. Sift together the dry ingredients and add to batter. Add drained apricots and chopped nuts, if they are used, then orange juice and mix well. Bake in loaf pan in medium oven—350° F or 175° C—about 50 minutes.

## BANANA BREAD

| | | |
|---|---|---|
| 1¾ cups | (4½ dl) | flour |
| 2½ tsp | (2½ tsp) | baking powder |
| ½ tsp | (½ tsp) | baking soda |
| 1 tsp | (1 tsp) | salt |
| ¾ cup | (1¾ dl) | sugar |
| ⅓ cup | (75 g) | butter or margarine |
| 2 | (2) | eggs |
| 1 tsp | | vanilla extract *or* |
| | (2 tsp) | vanilla sugar |
| 3 | (3) | bananas, well ripened |

Sift together the first four ingredients twice, cream sugar and butter, add eggs and beat until batter is smooth and fluffy. Mash bananas with a fork and stir into batter, add vanilla and then dry sifted ingredients, a little at a time, stirring constantly. Pour into loaf pan, and bake in medium oven—350° F or 175° C—about 50 minutes. Do not cut this cake until it is completely cool.

## DATE AND NUT LOAF

| | | |
|---|---|---|
| 1⅔ cups | (4 dl) | boiling water |
| 1⅔ cups | (4 dl) | dates, cut up into bits |
| ½ cup | (1¼ dl) | brown sugar |
| 1 tbsp | (1 tbsp) | butter or margarine |
| 1 | (1) | egg |
| 2 cups | (5 dl) | sifted flour |
| 1 tsp | (1 tsp) | baking soda |
| ½ tsp | (½ tsp) | salt |
| 1 cup, scant | (2 dl) | chopped nuts |

Pour boiling water over the dates and let cool. Cream brown sugar, butter and egg until fluffy. Add date mixture and sifted flour, mixed with baking soda and salt. Stir in chopped nuts and pour batter in greased, floured loaf pan. Let stand for 20 minutes *before* baking. Bake in medium oven—350° F or 175° C—60-70 minutes.

## PRUNE LOAF

| | | |
|---|---|---|
| 1⅔ cups | (4 dl) | water |
| 1⅔ cups | (4 dl) | prunes |
| | (about ¼ kg) | |
| 2 cups | (5 dl) | flour |
| 1 tsp | (1 tsp) | baking soda |
| ½ tsp | (½ tsp) | salt |
| 1 | (1) | egg |
| 2 tbsp | (2 tbsp) | salad oil or melted butter |

Bring prunes to boil in water, turn down heat and cook slowly for 10 minutes. Sift together flour, sugar, baking soda and salt and set aside. Pour off juice from prunes into a bowl, take out pits and chop fruit. Put this back into juice and measure same, it should be 2 cups (5 dl) and if it should be a little less, add water to make this quantity. Beat egg and butter or oil in a large bowl, add prune mixture and stir until well blended, then add flour mixture and mix well. Pour batter into a loaf pan, greased only on the bottom, and bake in medium oven—350° F or 175° C—50-60 minutes. Test with a toothpick to make sure cake is baked. Let cool in pan for

10 minutes before taking it out, then put it on a rack to cool. When fully cool, wrap loaf in plastic or aluminum foil and keep it in refrigerator overnight, before cutting it.

## BASIC YELLOW CAKE

| | | |
|---|---|---|
| 2 cups | (5 dl) | flour |
| 1⅔ cups | (4 dl) | sugar |
| 3 tsp | (3 tsp) | baking powder |
| 1 tsp | (1 tsp) | salt |
| ½ cup | (110 g) | butter or margarine |
| ⅔ cup | (1½ dl) | milk |
| 1 tsp | | vanilla extract *or* |
| | (2 tsp) | vanilla sugar |
| 2 | (2) | eggs plus an additional |
| ¼ cup | (½ dl) | milk |

Sift together all the dry ingredients and add butter or margarine which should be soft and at room temperature, then add milk and mix well. Beat eggs with the additional ¼ cup (½ dl) milk, add to mixture and beat until thick and fluffy. Pour batter into two round baking pans, about 8″ (20 cm) in diameter and bake 25–30

Basic Yellow Cake with lemon frosting

Sponge Cake cooling on a bottle

minutes in medium-hot oven—375° F or 190° C. Spread with frosting when cakes have cooled, both in between, around and on top. Mocha frosting or any cooked frosting is suitable for this cake.

## SILVER LAYER CAKE

| | | |
|---|---|---|
| 2½ cups | (6 dl) | flour |
| 1⅔ cups | (4 dl) | sugar |
| 3 tsp | (3 tsp) | baking powder |
| 1 tsp | (1 tsp) | salt |
| ½ cup | (110 g) | butter or margarine |
| ¾ cup | (1¾ dl) | milk |
| 1 tsp | | vanilla extract *or* |
| | (2 tsp) | vanilla sugar |
| 3 | (3) | egg whites |
| ¼ cup | (½ dl) | milk |

Sift together all the dry ingredients, add butter or margarine which should be soft and at room temperature, and ¾ cup (1¾ dl) milk and mix well. Add egg whites, mixed with remaining ¼ cup (½ dl) milk and beat vigorously until mixture is thick and fluffy. Pour batter into two baking pans, about 8″ (20 cm) in diameter and bake in medium oven—350° F or 175° C—about 30 minutes. Let cakes cool on rack, then fill with lemon filling and spread with frosting. Boiled frosting with coconut is suitable for this cake.

# FLUFFY SPONGE CAKE

| | | |
|---|---|---|
| 6 | (6) | eggs |
| 1½ cups | (4 dl) | sugar |
| ½ cup, scant | (1 dl) | cold water |
| 1 tsp | | vanilla extract *or* |
| | (1 tbsp) | vanilla sugar |
| 1 tbsp | (1 tbsp) | lemon juice |
| 1½ cups | (4 dl) | flour |
| 2 tsp | (2 tsp) | baking powder |
| 1 tsp | (1 tsp) | salt |

Separate eggs and beat egg yolks until lemon colored and thick, then add sugar little by little. Sift together flour, baking powder and salt and add to egg mixture alternately with the water. Add vanilla and lemon juice, then fold carefully in the egg whites which first have been beaten until stiff. Pour batter into an *ungreased* large ring pan and bake in slow oven—325° F or 160° C—about 1 hour or until the top springs back when lightly touched with tip of finger. After pan has been taken out of the oven, it is hung upside down on a bottle (see illustration) until it is completely cool. The cake can be eaten plain, or be spread with whipped cream (which can be mixed with some mashed fresh or frozen strawberries) or frosting.

# ANGEL FOOD CAKE

| | | |
|---|---|---|
| 12 | (12) | egg whites |
| 1 cup | (2½ dl) | sugar |
| 1 cup | (2½ dl) | flour |
| 2 tsp | (2 tsp) | baking powder |
| 1½ cups | (4 dl) | confectioners' sugar |
| ½ tsp | (½ tsp) | salt |
| 1 tsp | | vanilla extract *or* |
| | (1 tbsp) | vanilla sugar |

Beat egg whites until stiff, then add sugar, 2 tbsp at a time beating constantly until meringue holds stiff peaks. Sift together flour, confectioners' sugar, baking powder and salt at least three times and add carefully to meringue by folding in. Add vanilla and pour batter into an *ungreased* large ring pan. Gently cut through batter with a knife so that large air bubbles will disappear. Bake in medium warm oven—375° or 190° C—30–35 minutes or until cake top springs back when lightly touched by tip of finger. When pan has been taken out of oven, hang it upside down on a bottle until completely cool (see illustration on page 26) so that gravity will keep the texture light. This cake is rather difficult to cut with a knife and it is preferable to pull it apart with one or two broad forks. The cake may be served as it is, or spread with frosting or whipped cream.

## STRAWBERRY OR PEACH SHORTCAKE

*Here is a recipe for a dessert which is a top favorite for summer. It is not at all like the cakes used for this purpose in Europe, as it contains very little sugar. You must keep in mind, however, to be very liberal with the berries or the fruit if you want shortcake at its best.*

| 2 cups | (5 dl) | flour |
| 2 tbsp | (2 tbsp) | sugar |
| 4 tsp | (4 tsp) | baking powder |
| 1 tsp | (1 tsp) | salt |

Strawberry Shortcake

| ⅓ cup | (¾ dl) | shortening (see page 7) |
| 1 cup | (2½ dl) | milk |
| 1–2 quarts | (1–2 l) | strawberries or peaches |
| ½ cup | (1 dl) | sugar (more if fruit is acid) |
| 1 cup | (2½ dl) | whipping cream |

Sift together flour, sugar, baking powder and salt, then cut in shortening with two knives or a pastry blender, until a crumbly mixture (crumbs of the size of a small pea) is formed. Quickly mix in milk, stirring as little as possible. Spread batter in two baking pans (about 8″ or 20–22 cm in diameter) and flatten it out. Dot a little butter on top and bake in hot oven—450° F or 230° C—12–15 minutes. Put one cake upside down on a platter, spread with sugared chopped berries or fruit, then put the second cake, right side up, on top and heap additional berries or fruit on this. Whipped cream may be spread on top, or be served by itself in a bowl.

## MISSISSIPPI MUD

*Dark and moist chocolate cakes are very popular in the States. This one is surprisingly easy to make and is therefore a favorite among youngsters when they get the urge to bake.*

Black Devils' Cake with chocolate
frosting

**Mississippi Mud, continued**

| | | |
|---|---|---|
| 2 cups | (5 dl) | water |
| 4 squares | (200 g) | unsweetened chocolate *or* |
| ⅔ cup | (1½ dl) | cocoa, but then use larger quantity of butter |
| 2 cups | (5 dl) | sugar |
| 1-1½ cups | (200–250 g) | butter or margarine |
| 2 cups | (5 dl) | flour |
| 1 tsp | (1 tsp) | salt |
| 1 tsp | (1 tsp) | baking soda |
| 2 | (2) | eggs, slightly beaten |

Bring water to a boil, add chocolate or cocoa and let it come to a boil and cook for about one minute. Add sugar and butter or margarine. Let mixture cool. Sift together flour, baking soda and salt and add to the cooled chocolate mixture. Stir in the two slightly beaten eggs and mix well. Bake in a greased and floured loaf pan in slow oven—about 300–325° F or 150–160° C—about 1½ hours.

## BLACK DEVILS' FOOD CAKE

| | | |
|---|---|---|
| ½ cup | (1¼ dl) | cocoa |
| 1 cup | (2½ dl) | strong, hot coffee |
| 1½ cups | (4 dl) | flour |
| 1 tsp | (1 tsp) | salt |
| 1 tsp | (1 tsp) | baking soda |
| ½ tsp | (½ tsp) | baking powder |
| ½ cup | (110 g) | butter or margarine |
| 1¼ cups | (3 dl) | sugar |
| 2 | (2) | eggs |
| 1 tsp | | vanilla extract *or* |
| | (2 tsp) | vanilla sugar |

Mix cocoa and coffee. Cream sugar and butter or margarine, add eggs, one at a time and stir well after each addition. Sift together flour, baking soda, baking powder and salt and add to butter and egg mixture alternately with the cocoa mixture and beat until smooth. Bake in two baking pans, about 8″ in diameter (20 cm) in medium oven—350° F or 175° C—45–50 minutes. Let cakes cool and spread with frosting, in between and all over cake. Either mocha frosting or boiled frosting with coconut is good with this cake.

## BASIC UNCOOKED BUTTER FROSTING

*When people in other lands think of American cakes, it is most often of those covered with frosting. This is a thick, sweet covering, usually soft, and flavored in different ways. Here are a few different varieties, some easily made and some a little more complicated.*

| ⅓ cup | (75 g) | butter or margarine |
|-------|--------|---------------------|
| 3 cups | (7 dl) | confectioners' sugar |
| ¼ cup | (½ dl) | light cream or milk |
| 1 tsp | | vanilla extract *or* |
| | (2 tsp) | vanilla sugar |

Cream butter or margarine until fluffy, then add confectioners' sugar, vanilla, and milk, beating until very smooth and fluffy. If mixture should turn out too thin, add a little more confectioners' sugar. Mixture should be easy to spread with a knife. This recipe is about right to cover two 8″ (20 cm diameter) layers.

**Variations:**

LEMON OR ORANGE FROSTING
Instead of milk or cream add ¼ cup (½ dl) lemon or orange juice. Also add 1 tsp grated lemon or orange rind.

STRAWBERRY FROSTING
Instead of milk or cream, use ¼ cup (½ dl) mashed strawberries.

MOCHA FROSTING
Instead of milk or cream add ¼ cup (½ dl) cocoa and ¼ cup (½ dl) strong coffee.

CHOCOLATE FROSTING
Instead of milk or cream, use 2 egg yolks and scant ½ cup of cocoa.

LIQUEUR FROSTING
Instead of milk or cream use ¼ cup (½ dl) of your favorite liqueur or the one you happen to have on hand.

## BASIC BOILED FROSTING

| | | |
|---|---|---|
| 1¼ cups | (3 dl) | sugar |
| | | pinch of salt |
| ⅓ cup | (¾ dl) | water |
| 3 | (3) | egg whites |
| 1 tsp | | vanilla extract *or* |
| | (2 tsp) | vanilla sugar |

Mix sugar, salt and water in a heavy sauce pan and stir over low heat until sugar is dissolved. Let mixture cook until it reaches 240° F or 130° C, when one drop of it will form a hard ball when dropped in cold water. Remove from heat. Beat egg whites until stiff and add sugar mixture in a thin stream to meringue, beating constantly. Add vanilla and continue beating until mixture is very fluffy and holds stiff peaks. Spread immediately on cake and spread shredded coconut or chopped nuts etc. on top, if desired. This recipe frosts two cake layers of about 8″ (20 cm) diameter.

**Variation:**

LADY BALTIMORE FROSTING
To ⅓ of the above frosting add ¼ cup (½ dl) candied, chopped cherries, ¼ cup (½ dl) chopped raisins and ½ cup (1 dl) chopped

Basic Yellow Cake with chocolate frosting, Black and White Striped Cake with liqueur frosting

nuts and 1 tsp grated orange or lemon peel. Spread this mixture in between cake and use the plain frosting for rest of cake.

## BLACK AND WHITE STRIPED CAKE

Make half a batch each of Basic Yellow or Silver Cake and Black Devils Food Cake and cut each cake layer in two halves horizontally. Then put alternating layers of the light and dark cakes. Frost in between layers and on top and around cake using Liqueur Frosting, preferably made with cacao liqueur.

## SILHOUETTE CAKE

For this cake use 30 thin ginger cookies or chocolate cookies. Whip 1 cup (2 dl) heavy cream and add 2 tbsp confectioners' sugar. Spread a little whipped cream on one cooky, place one on top, spread cream on this one and continue until you get a pile of five cookies. Make six of these piles. Lay the piles on their sides in one or two rows and cover them evenly with remaining cream. Chill in refrigerator at least five hours before it is cut.

On birthdays etc. you may arrange the cookies so that they will form a number, see illustration below.

Silhouette Cake

## PINEAPPLE UPSIDE DOWN CAKE

| | | |
|---|---|---|
| 6–8 slices | (6–8 slices) | canned or fresh pineapple |
| ¼ cup | (60 g) | butter or margarine |
| ¾ cup | (1¾ dl) | brown sugar |
| 6–8 | (6–8) | maraschino cherries |
| 8 | (8) | pecan or walnut halves |
| 1 cup | (2½ dl) | flour |
| ¾ cup | (1¾ dl) | sugar |
| 2 tsp | (2 tsp) | baking powder |
| ½ tsp | (½ tsp) | salt |
| ¼ cup | (60 g) | butter or margarine, melted |
| ⅔ cup | (1½ dl) | milk |
| 1 | (1) | egg |
| 2 tbsp | (2 tbsp) | pineapple juice |

Melt ¼ cup (60 g) butter in an iron skillet over low heat. Add brown sugar and stir until melted. Remove from heat. Arrange well drained pineapple slices in a nice pattern on top of melted sugar; place a cherry in the middle of each slice and the nut halves in a design around. In a bowl sift together flour, sugar, baking powder and salt. Add melted butter and milk and mix well. Add egg and pineapple juice. When all is well blended, pour batter carefully on top of pineapple slices in skillet and bake cake in medium oven—350° F or 175° C—40–45 minutes. When cake is ready, let it stand a few minutes in pan before it is carefully turned upside down. Serve either warm, with whipped cream, or cold with coffee or tea.

## COCOA BROWNIES

*Brownies are bar cookies with a soft and chewy consistency. They are about the most popular baked sweet in American homes. Most of them are eaten informally, but they are delicious served with coffee or tea, or as a dessert.*

| | | |
|---|---|---|
| 1 cup | (2½ dl) | flour |
| 1 cup | (2½ dl) | sugar |
| ⅓ tsp | (⅓ tsp) | salt |

| ⅓ cup | (¾ dl) | cocoa |
| ½ cup | (110 g) | butter or margarine |
| 3 | (3) | eggs |
| 1 tsp | | vanilla extract *or* |
| | (1 tbsp) | vanilla sugar |
| ½ cup, scant | (1 dl) | chopped almonds or other nuts |

Sift together the first four ingredients. Cream butter and add the dry ingredients. Mix in eggs, one at a time, add vanilla and nuts. Pour batter in a greased baking pan and even it out to about ½″ deep. Bake in slow oven—325° F or 160° C—20-25 minutes. If desired, additional nuts can be sprinkled on top of batter before baking. When ready, let pan stand about 10 minutes before cake is cut up into bars.

## CHOCOLATE BROWNIES

| 1 cup | (2½ dl) | sugar |
| 2 | (2) | eggs |
| ½ cup | (1¼ dl) | flour |
| 6 tbsp | (70 g) | butter or margarine |
| 2 squares | (50 g) | unsweetened chocolate |
| 1 tsp | | vanilla extract *or* |
| | (1 tbsp) | vanilla sugar |
| About ½ cup | (1 dl) | walnuts or almonds, if desired |

Beat sugar and eggs until fluffy. Melt butter and chocolate over hot water, or *very low* heat and add to egg mixture alternately with sifted flour. Chop nuts or almonds and add together with vanilla. Bake preferably in square pan—about 8 x 8″ (20 x 20 cm)—in medium oven—350° F or 175° C—20-25 minutes. Let stand for about 10 minutes before cutting up into bars.

## TOFFEE ALMOND BARS

| ½ cup | (110 g) | butter or margarine |
| ½ cup | (1¼ dl) | brown sugar |
| 1 cup | (2½ dl) | flour |

Cream butter and sugar until fluffy, add flour and spread mixture in an ungreased baking pan, about 8 x 12″ (20 x 30 cm). Bake for about 10 minutes in medium oven—350° F or 175° C. Remove from oven and spread with the following topping:

| | | |
|---|---|---|
| 2 | (2) | eggs |
| 1 cup | (2½ dl) | brown sugar |
| ½ tsp | | vanilla extract, *or* |
| | (1 tsp) | vanilla sugar |
| 2 tbsp | (2 tbsp) | flour |
| 1 tsp | (1 tsp) | baking powder |
| ½ tsp | (½ tsp) | salt |
| 1 cup | (2½ dl) | shredded coconut |
| 1 cup | (2½ dl) | chopped almonds |

Beat eggs until fluffy. Mix in brown sugar and vanilla, add flour mixed with baking powder and salt. Stir in coconut and almonds and spread mixture evenly on partly baked cake and put back in the oven. Bake an additional 25 minutes, or until top has a golden color. Let it cool somewhat before it is cut up into bars.

## BUTTERSCOTCH BROWNIES

| | | |
|---|---|---|
| ½ cup | (60 g) | butter or margarine |
| ½ cup | (1¼ dl) | brown sugar |
| 1 | (1) | egg |
| 1 cup, scant | (2 dl) | flour |
| 1 tsp | (1 tsp) | baking powder |
| ½ tsp | (½ tsp) | salt |
| 1 tsp | | vanilla extract *or* |
| | (1 tbsp) | vanilla sugar |
| ½ cup, scant | (1 dl) | chopped almonds or other nuts |

Melt butter over low heat, remove from heat and let it cool somewhat. Stir in brown sugar and egg and beat. Sift together flour, baking powder and salt and add to batter. Add vanilla and chopped almonds or nuts. Spread batter in a square baking pan, about 8 x 8″ (20 x 20 cm) or a 9″ (22 cm) round pan. Bake in medium oven—350° F or 175° C—about 25 minutes. Let cake stand for about 5–10 minutes before cutting it into bars.

Various types of brownies

## PEANUT BUTTER BROWNIES

| | | |
|---|---|---|
| 2 | (2) | eggs |
| 1 cup | (2½ dl) | sugar |
| ½ cup | (1¼ dl) | brown sugar |
| ¼ cup | (½ dl) | peanut butter |
| 2 tbsp | (2 tbsp) | butter or margarine |
| ½ tsp | | vanilla extract *or* |
| | (1 tsp) | vanilla sugar |
| 1¼ cups | (3 dl) | flour |
| 2 tsp | (2 tsp) | baking powder |
| ½ tsp | (½ tsp) | salt |
| 2 tbsp | (2 tbsp) | chopped peanuts |

Combine eggs, sugar, brown sugar, peanut butter, butter or margarine and vanilla and mix ingredients well. Add flour, mixed with baking powder and salt, and beat until batter is smoothly blended. Spread in a square baking pan—about 8 x 8″ (20 x 20 cm)—or a 9″ (22 cm) round pan, and sprinkle chopped peanuts on top. Bake in medium oven—350° F or 175° C—about 30 minutes. Let stand in pan for about 5 minutes, then cut cake into bars.

# OATMEAL COOKIES

*Most American housewives do not seem to have the interest or patience to make the beautifully shaped and decorated cookies which are the pride of so many Europeans. They prefer those made from softer batter that can be dropped by spoonfuls on the baking pans, so that rolling and cutting are not needed. These drop cookies are delicious, too.*

| | | |
|---|---|---|
| ⅔ cup | (1½ dl) | brown sugar |
| ½ cup | (1¼ dl) | sugar (white) |
| ½ cup | (110 g) | butter or margarine |
| 1 | (1) | egg |
| 1 tsp | | vanilla extract *or* |
| | (2 tsp) | vanilla sugar |
| 1 tbsp | (1 tbsp) | milk |
| 1 cup | (2½ dl) | flour |
| ½ tsp | (½ tsp) | baking soda |
| ½ tsp | (½ tsp) | baking powder |
| ½ tsp | (½ tsp) | salt |
| 1 cup | (2½ dl) | quick-cooking oatmeal |

Blend brown and white sugar, butter, egg, vanilla and milk and stir vigorously until mixture is smooth. Sift together flour, baking powder, baking soda and salt and add to egg mixture, and blend well. Stir in oatmeal and blend. Drop dough by teaspoonfuls on greased baking plate about 2″ (5 cm) apart. Bake in medium oven—350° F or 175° C—12 minutes or until cookies are golden brown. Makes about 3 dozen cookies.

# OATMEAL SPICE COOKIES

| | | |
|---|---|---|
| ¾ cup | (125 g) | butter or margarine |
| 1 cup | (2½ dl) | sugar |
| 1 | (1) | egg |
| 1½ cups | (3½ dl) | flour |
| 1 tsp | (1 tsp) | baking soda |
| ½ tsp | (½ tsp) | salt |
| ½ tsp | (½ tsp) | ginger |
| ¼ tsp | (¼ tsp) | ground cloves |
| ¼ cup | (½ dl) | molasses |
| ⅔ cup | (1½ dl) | quick-cooking oatmeal |

Cream sugar with butter or margarine until fluffy, then add egg. Sift together flour, baking soda, salt and spices and add to egg mixture alternately with the molasses. Blend well. Stir in oats and drop by teaspoonfuls on greased baking plate, rather far apart as the cookies spread during baking. Bake in warm oven—400° F or 200° C—8–10 minutes.

## COCONUT OATMEAL COOKIES

| | | |
|---|---|---|
| ¾ cup | (125 g) | butter or margarine |
| ⅔ cup | (1½ dl) | sugar |
| ⅔ cup | (1½ dl) | brown sugar |
| 1 | (1) | egg, slightly beaten |
| 1 tsp | | vanilla extract *or* |
| | (1 tbsp) | vanilla sugar |
| 1¼ cups | (3 dl) | flour |
| 1 tsp | (1 tsp) | baking powder |
| 1 tsp | (1 tsp) | baking soda |
| 1 tsp | (1 tsp) | salt |
| ⅔ cup | (1½ dl) | quick-cooking oatmeal |
| 1 cup | (2 dl) | shredded coconut |

Cream sugar and butter until smooth, then add slightly beaten egg. Sift together flour, baking powder, baking soda and salt and add to egg mixture, a little at a time, stirring constantly until smooth. Add vanilla, then oatmeal and coconut, blend well, and drop by teaspoonfuls on a greased baking sheet. Bake in medium-warm oven—375–400° F or 190–200° C—10–12 minutes or until cookies are golden brown.

## ALMOND CRESCENTS

| ¾ cup | (125 g) | butter or margarine |
|---|---|---|
| 4 | (4) | grated bitter almonds *or* |
| ½ tsp | (½ tsp) | almond extract |
| 1 tsp | | vanilla extract *or* |
| | (2 tsp) | vanilla sugar |
| ½ cup | (1 dl) | sugar |
| ½ cup, scant | (1 dl) | ground almonds |
| 1 cup, appr | (2–2½ dl) | flour |
| ¼ cup | (½ dl) | confectioners' sugar |

Cream sugar, butter or margarine until fluffy. Add vanilla, bitter almonds and ground almonds. Add sifted flour and mix well. Put dough on floured board and knead until it is smooth and holds together. Divide dough into two parts and roll each one into two long rolls, about 1–1½″ (2–3 cm) thick. Cut these rolls into pieces of ¼–½″ (1–1½ cm) each. Roll each piece in your hands and form crescents which are then put on an ungreased baking sheet. It is safer to make a test cooky first, before all crescents are formed, and if this test cooky loses its shape by flattening out too much, add a little bit more flour. Bake in medium oven—350° F or 175° C—about 20 minutes. Let them cool somewhat and sprinkle with confectioners' sugar.

## PINEAPPLE COOKIES

| ½ cup | (110 g) | butter or margarine |
|---|---|---|
| 1 cup | (2½ dl) | sugar |
| 1 | (1) | egg, slightly beaten |
| ¾ cup | (1¾ dl) | crushed pineapple |
| 2 cups | (5 dl) | flour |
| ½ tsp | (½ tsp) | baking soda |
| 1 tsp | (1 tsp) | baking powder |
| ½ tsp | (½ tsp) | salt |
| 1 tsp | | vanilla extract *or* |
| | (1 tbsp) | vanilla sugar |
| ½ cup, scant | (1 dl) | chopped walnuts (or almonds) |

Cream butter and sugar until fluffy, add egg. Sift together the dry ingredients and add to batter. Stir in pineapple and chopped nuts. Bake a test cooky by dropping a teaspoonful of dough on a greased baking plate and bake in medium oven—350° F or 175° C—about 12 minutes. If the test cooky should flatten out too much, add a little more flour to dough, but if cooky holds a nice shape, drop the rest of dough by teaspoonfuls on plate and bake. These cookies are moist and keep well in an air tight container—but find a hiding place too, if you have a family that loves good cookies.

## RUMBALLS

| | | |
|---|---|---|
| 1 cup | (2½ dl) | crushed vanilla wafers |
| 1 cup | (2½ dl) | confectioners' sugar |
| 1¼ cups | (3 dl) | chopped nuts or almonds |
| 2 tbsp | (2 tbsp) | cocoa |
| 2 tbsp | (2 tbsp) | corn syrup |
| ¼ cup | (½ dl) | rum |

Crush vanilla wafers (easily done by putting them in a plastic bag and rolling with a rolling pin or a bottle), mix with the sugar, nuts and cocoa. Add syrup and rum. Shape small, round balls, about ¾″ (2 cm) in diameter and roll same in additional confectioners' sugar or chopped nuts. Keep in air tight container. They also keep very well in the freezer and can then be taken out as needed. Instead of rum you can use whisky, or creme de cacao, but if the latter is used, lessen the amount of sugar slightly.

## ONE CRUST PIE SHELL

*This is a standard recipe for pie crust. Here, and wherever pie crust is mentioned in this book, it is meant for a standard American pie pan, which is round with sloped sides and is 9 inches (about 23 cm) in top inside diameter, and nearly 2 inches (5 cm) narrower at the bottom. If baking is done in a different size or type of pan, quantities may have to be changed.*

*Pie Fillings and complete pies are described under DESSERTS, pages 143 to 156.*

## One Crust Pie Shell, continued

| | | |
|---|---|---|
| 1 cup | (2½ dl) | flour |
| ½ tsp | (½ tsp) | salt |
| ⅓ cup | (1 dl) | shortening (preferably vegetable shortening such as Spry or Crisco, but lard can also be used. Butter or margarine (75 g) may also be used but the crust will not be as crisp with this.) |
| 2–3 tbsp | (2–3 tbsp) | ice-cold water |

Sift flour and salt into a bowl, add shortening and cut with a pastry cutter or two knives until the mixture consists of crumbs the size of a pea. Sprinkle water over and stir lightly with a fork until mixture is evenly moist. Take the ball of dough in your hand and scrape with it around the edges of the bowl in order to get all crumbs and press all of it together into a ball. You can roll this out immediately, or put it in a refrigerator for a while to get cool

Pie crust is cut
Pie crust folded and placed in pan
Edge is decorated by pinching
Edge is decorated with a fork

first. Do *not,* however, knead dough on baking board, as crust will then not be as crisp. After dough has been rolled out, put the pie pan on top and with a cutter or knife, cut about 1″ (2 cm) beyond pie pan. Fold pie pastry in half, and this once more in half (that is into four parts), put into pie pan and unfold. Trim edges and make a nice edge (see illustration). Just before pie crust is put into the oven, prick it with a fork and brush with melted butter. Bake in hot oven—450° F or 230° C—about 8 minutes, if the pie crust is going to be used already baked, otherwise fill it with the proper filling and bake in the temperature which is mentioned for the recipe in question.

## TWO CRUST PIE SHELL

| | | |
|---|---|---|
| 2 cups | (5 dl) | flour |
| 1 tsp | (1 tsp) | salt |
| ⅔ cup | (2 dl) | **shortening (preferably vegetable shortening such as Spry or Crisco, but lard can also be used. Butter or margarine (150 g) may also be used but the crust will not be as crisp with this).** |
| ¼ cup | (½ dl) | ice-cold water |

Proceed in the same manner as for One Crust Pie Shell but roll out only half of the dough and put into pie pan. After the filling

to be used has been added, make a "cover" by rolling out remaining dough. Cut a design near the center to let steam out. Let cover overlap the lower crust, and pinch edges together, so that they will not open, and then decorate edges as the illustration shows.

## GRAHAM CRACKER CRUST

| | | |
|---|---|---|
| 1¼ cups | (3 dl) | graham cracker crumbs |
| 2 tbsp | (2 tbsp) | sugar |
| ⅓ cup | (60 g) | butter or margarine, melted |

Mix together all ingredients and pour mixture into pie pan. Press mixture against the sides and bottom in an even layer with a spoon or with hand. Bake in medium oven—350° F or 175° C—about ten minutes. Let cool and then put in the proper filling. This type of crust is suitable for chiffon pies and cream pies.

A variation of this pie crust can be made by using crumbs of chocolate cookies or ginger cookies instead.

# MAIN DISHES

It has been extremely difficult to choose main dishes from among the too-large number which I have had in mind to represent the accomplishments of the American kitchen. Testing eliminated a few, mostly on the basis of difficult or complicated preparation, but occasionally because of questions of taste or appearance.

Many more were eliminated because they were too similar to dishes that were already popular in the countries being studied. Since the original edition of this book was written in Swedish for Sweden, particular attention was paid to duplication in northern Europe.

The recipes that are included are therefore those that are both typically American and different from food customarily prepared in other countries. Also, they are all reasonably easy to prepare without special kitchen equipment.

Casseroles are of many kinds. They are particularly useful when serving guests in homes without household help, which are typical in the United States and are becoming more common throughout most of the world. Most casseroles can be prepared partly or completely ahead of time, so that the hostess can spend most of her time with her guests instead of in the kitchen.

You may wonder why this book has so many recipes for tuna. For one thing, canned tuna seems to be available over a large part of the world, and it lends itself well to preparation of many dishes that are both delicious and economical. Also, it was tuna that gave me the idea of writing this book. On a visit to Sweden I commented on the fact that I had seen it on the shelves of several stores, and was told that it was a mystery how Americans used it so much, as it did not taste very good. I found that it was just being eaten directly out of the can, in the same manner as Swedish herring. I have to admit that you would have to really like tuna to enjoy it that way.

Chicken is also well represented. It has always been an American favorite, and it has become quite economical in comparison to other meats.

## BAKED STUFFED COD

*American fish cooking is usually rather plain—fish is just boiled, baked or fried. But baked fish may also be stuffed, and this stuffing is somewhat different from that used in Europe. Cod is not always available in the tropics, but red snapper is also excellent served this way.*

| | | |
|---|---|---|
| 1 | (1) | cod, about 3 lbs |
| 4 tbsp | (4 tbsp) | butter or margarine |
| 1 | (1) | small finely chopped onion |
| 1 cup | (2½ dl) | white bread, cut into small cubes |
| ⅓ tsp | (⅓ tsp) | thyme |
| ¼ tsp | (¼ tsp) | sage |
| 1 tbsp | (1 tbsp) | minced parsley |
| 1 | (1) | hard boiled egg, chopped |
| | | salt and pepper |
| ⅓ cup | (¾ dl) | milk or water |
| 4 | (4) | slices salt pork |

Rub fish over with one tablespoon melted butter seasoned with a little pepper and salt. Heat the remaining butter in a saucepan and cook the onion in it until wilted, stirring frequently. Add bread cubes, seasonings and flavorings with the egg and moisten with milk or water, but use only enough to soften the cubes without making them wet. Stuff the fish with this dressing and sew or skewer the cavity. Put the salt pork in a baking dish, put the fish on top and pour about ⅔ cup water (1½ dl) into the pan. Bake in medium oven—350° F or 175° C—about 45 minutes and baste in the meantime with the liquid in the pan, adding a little more if necessary. Serve on hot platter and garnish with lemon slices and parsley. Serves six.

# BAKED FISH WITH PAPRIKA

*This is quick and easy to prepare, and provides something a little different from ordinary baked fish.*

| | | |
|---|---|---|
| 1 | (1) | large onion, cut into thin slices |
| 2 tbsp | (2 tbsp) | butter or margarine |
| 1½ lbs | (¾ kg) | fresh or frozen fish fillets (cod, haddock or other salt water fish) |
| ¾ cup | (2 dl) | milk and cream mixed |
| 1 tbsp | (1 tbsp) | paprika |
| 1 tsp | (1 tsp) | salt |
| | | pinch of pepper |

Cook onion in butter or margarine until golden brown, but make sure it does not become dark brown. Spread onion slices in the bottom of a low baking dish, cut fish in serving pieces and place on top of onion. Beat remaining ingredients lightly and pour over fish. Bake in medium oven—350° F or 175° C—about 25 minutes. Makes 4–5 servings.

# FISH CAKES

*A nice variation in preparing salt fish, which makes an asset out of its strong flavor.*

| | | |
|---|---|---|
| ½ lb | (3 hg) | salt cod or ling |
| 3 | (3) | large potatoes, sliced (about 2 cups—5 dl) |
| 1 tsp | (1 tsp) | dry mustard |
| 1 tbsp | (1 tbsp) | minced onion |
| 2 tsp | (2 tsp) | lemon juice |
| 1 | (1) | egg, slightly beaten |
| 2 tsp | (2 tsp) | salt |
| | | flour |

Cut salt fish into small pieces, rinse in warm water, place in bowl, then pour boiling water over it and let stand three minutes. Drain and shred fish. Boil fish and potatoes until potatoes are tender, drain and dry over low heat. Mash them, add the remaining ingredients except flour, form either balls or cakes, dip or roll them in flour and fry in butter or margarine until golden brown, about 2 minutes. Serves six.

## FISH CHOWDER

*This is a hearty and nourishing soup that is suitable for a main dish on chilly days. It comes from New England, where it is considered to be a relation of clam chowder. Clams, which are a specially-flavored relative of mussels, are difficult to obtain in many parts of the world. If you can get them, fresh, canned or frozen, you can substitute them for fish in this recipe, using half the quantity.*

| | | |
|---|---|---|
| 2 lbs | (1 kg) | fresh cod or haddock |
| ½ cup | (about 1 hg) | salt pork, cut into small cubes |
| 2 | (2) | medium onions, sliced |
| 4 | (4) | large potatoes, cut into cubes |
| 1 cup | (2 dl) | chopped celery |
| 1 | (1) | bay leaf |
| 1 quart | (1 l) | milk |
| 1 quart | (1 l) | water |
| 2 tbsp | (2 tbsp) | butter |
| 1 tsp | (1 tsp) | salt |
| ½ tsp | (½ tsp) | pepper |

Simmer fish in 2 cups (5 dl) water about 15 minutes. Drain and reserve liquid. Fry pork cubes until crisp, remove and reserve. Sauté onion in pork fat, pour into a large sauce pan and add potatoes, celery, spices, 1 cup (2½ dl) broth from fish and 2 cups (5 dl) boiling water. Simmer for about 15 minutes and add fish, broken into bite-size pieces. Bring to a boil, add milk and butter and heat until *almost* boiling but no further. Just before serving, add pork cubes and sprinkle with chopped parsley. Serves six.

## CURRIED TUNA WITH EGGS

*Canned tuna fish is kept on hand in most American kitchens in 7 oz (2 hg) cans, and has found its way to grocery store shelves in many countries. Tuna provides a pleasing base for a large number of different dishes and salads, most of which are easy and quick to make. Can you imagine anything handier to prepare in a hurry than the following?*

| 2 tbsp | (2 tbsp) | butter |
|---|---|---|
| 2 tbsp | (2 tbsp) | flour |
| 1½–2 cups | (4–5 dl) | milk |
| 1–2 tsp | (1–2 tsp) | curry |
| 5 | (5) | hard boiled eggs |
| 1 can | (1 can) | tuna |
| | | pepper and salt to taste |

Melt butter in a saucepan, stir in flour and then milk, a little at a time, stirring constantly to make a smooth sauce. Flavor with salt, pepper and curry, dissolved in a little water. Cut eggs in rather big pieces and add these, then add tuna also broken up into rather big pieces. Serve with rice or over toast.

## TUNA CASSEROLE WITH SPAGHETTI

| 1 can | (1 can) | tuna |
|---|---|---|
| 1 | (1) | clove of garlic, minced *or* ½ onion, minced |
| 4 | (4) | large tomatoes, peeled and quartered (or 1 can tomatoes), about 2 cups (½ l) |
| 1 tsp | (1 tsp) | sugar |
| 1 tbsp | (1 tbsp) | minced parsley |
| 8 | (8) | olives, sliced (black, green or stuffed) |
| ½ lb | (¼ kg) | spaghetti (to be cooked separately) |
| | | grated cheese to sprinkle over each portion, if desired |

Pour oil from tuna can into a heavy sauce pan and if onion is used, sauté in this for a few minutes. Break up tuna into small pieces, and add together with clove of garlic (if this is used), tomatoes, sugar and parsley. Cover and simmer gently until thickened. In case it should get too thick, add a little bouillon (made from bouillon cube if other is not available), or water. Just before serving add sliced olives and cooked, drained spaghetti. Serves 4–6.

## TUNA LOAF

*This tuna dish takes a little time to prepare, but it is well worth the trouble, as it is unusual, festive and tasty.*

| | | |
|---|---|---|
| 2 cups | (5 dl) | flour |
| ½ tsp | (½ tsp) | salt |
| 4 tsp | (4 tsp) | baking powder |
| ¼ cup | (60 g) | shortening, preferably vegetable shortening such as Spry or Crisco. Butter or margarine can also be used. |
| 1 | (1) | egg, slightly beaten |
| ½ cup | (1¼ dl) | milk |

Sift together flour, salt and baking powder, then cut in shortening with pastry cutter or two knives until a crumbly mixture with crumbs the size of a pea is obtained. Add slightly beaten egg and milk and shape dough into a ball, but work it as little as possible with your hands. Roll out immediately into a square, about 8 x 12″ (20 x 30 cm). On top of this put the following filling:

| | | |
|---|---|---|
| 1 can | (1 can) | tuna (or 2 cans, if desired) |
| 2 tbsp | (2 tbsp) | minced onion |
| ¼ cup | (½ dl) | milk |
| ½ tbsp | (½ tbsp) | minced parsley |
| ¼ cup | (½ dl) | chopped sweet pickles or dill pickles |
| ½ tsp | (½ tsp) | salt |

Break up tuna with a fork and add the other ingredients and mix well. After filling has been placed on dough, roll it together like a jelly roll, wet edges so that loaf will not open up during baking. Bake in warm oven—400° F or 200° C—about 30 minutes. Cut loaf immediately into thick slices and serve with cheese sauce (see page 166). Serves 4–5.

## RICE DEVILED EGG TUNA CASSEROLE

| | | |
|---|---|---|
| 2 tbsp | (2 tbsp) | butter or margarine |
| ¼ cup | (½ dl) | green pepper, chopped |
| ¼ cup | (½ dl) | minced onion |
| 1 can | (1 can) | cream of mushroom soup |
| 1 cup | (2½ dl) | milk |
| 2 cups | (5 dl) | boiled rice |
| 1 can | (1 can) | tuna |
| ¼ cup | (½ dl) | bread crumbs |
| ½ cup | (1 dl) | grated cheese, preferably Cheddar |

**Deviled Eggs:**

| | | |
|---|---|---|
| 4 | (4) | eggs, hardboiled |
| ½ tsp | (½ tsp) | dry mustard |
| | | pinch of salt |
| | | paprika |
| 2 tbsp | (2 tbsp) | mayonnaise |

Sauté onion and green pepper in butter until tender, add mushroom soup, milk, rice and tuna and mix well. Pour into a greased baking dish, place deviled eggs on top. Sprinkle bread crumbs and then grated cheese on top but take care not to sprinkle on top of eggs, but *around* them. Bake in medium oven—350° F or 175° C—about 20 minutes or until cheese is fully melted and the casserole has a golden color. Serves four.

**Deviled Eggs:**

Cut eggs lengthwise and remove egg yolks and place them in a bowl. Mash them and mix well with remaining ingredients, then put mixture carefully back into the egg whites.

## TUNA TETRAZZINI

| | | |
|---|---|---|
| 6 tbsp | (6 tbsp) | minced onion |
| 2 tbsp | (2 tbsp) | salad oil |
| 2 cans | (2 cans) | cream of mushroom soup |
| 1¼ cups | (3 dl) | water |
| ½ cup | (1 dl) | grated Parmesan cheese |
| 2 cans | (2 cans) | tuna |
| ⅔ cup | (1½ dl) | black olives, pitted and sliced |
| 2 tbsp | (2 tbsp) | minced parsley |
| 2 tsp | (2 tsp) | lemon juice |
| | | pinch each of thyme and marjoram |
| ½ lb | (¼ kg) | spaghetti |

Sauté onion in oil until golden and wilted. Add mushroom soup, mixed with water and ¼ cup (½ dl) of grated cheese. Break up tuna into rather large pieces and add to sauce together with olives, mix carefully and heat until thoroughly warm. Add parsley, lemon juice, thyme and marjoram. Cook spaghetti in salted water and drain. Mix with sauce and pour it all into a greased baking dish. Sprinkle remaining ¼ cup (½ dl) cheese on top and put under broiler until casserole is golden brown. Serves 6–8.

## TUNA CASSEROLE

| | | |
|---|---|---|
| 2 | (2) | eggs |
| | | pinch of salt and pepper |
| 2 cups | (5 dl) | soft bread crumbs (cut white bread into thin slices, then into small cubes) |
| 1¼ cups | (3 dl) | mayonnaise |
| 2 cans | (2 cans) | tuna |
| 1 pkg | (1 pkg) | frozen peas and carrots, cooked |
| 1 cup, scant | (2 dl) | chopped green pepper |
| 2 tbsp | (2 tbsp) | minced onion |
| 2 cups | (5 dl) | mashed potatoes |
| | | melted butter or margarine |

Separate eggs and beat yolks in a large bowl, add a pinch of salt and pepper. Mix in bread crumbs and ¾ cup (2 dl) mayonnaise. Drain tuna and break up into pieces and add to egg mixture, then add vegetables and pour into a greased baking dish. Flatten out mixture evenly and bake in medium oven—350° F or 175° C—until all is thoroughly hot, about 25 minutes. In the meantime beat egg whites until stiff, blend in ½ cup (1 dl) mayonnaise and spread this on top, but leave an edge of about 1″ (3 cm) all around. Place mashed potatoes around the edge in a nice design, brush with melted butter or margarine and put under broiler until the casserole is golden brown. Makes six servings.

## TUNA RICE PIE

| | | |
|---|---|---|
| 1¼ cups | (3 dl) | Minute rice |
| 1¼ cups | (3 dl) | water |
| 1 tsp | (1 tsp) | salt |
| 2 tsp | (2 tsp) | butter or margarine |
| 3 | (3) | eggs |
| 1 cup | (2½ dl) | grated cheese (preferably Cheddar) |
| 1 can | (1 can) | tuna |
| ⅔ cup | (1½ dl) | milk |
| | | pinch of nutmeg and pepper |

Put rice in a baking dish. Bring water, salt and butter to a boil and pour over rice and let stand for five minutes. Beat one egg slightly and stir with rice and press mixture against bottom and sides of dish. Sprinkle ½ cup (1 dl) grated cheese on top and spread half of tuna on this, then an additional layer each of cheese and tuna. Mix together two eggs, milk, salt, pepper and nutmeg and remaining cheese and pour over tuna mixture. Bake in hot

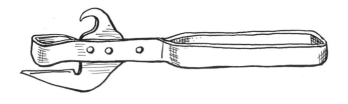

oven—400° F or 200° C—for about 25 minutes. If desired, tomato wedges can be put on top during the last 5 minutes of baking. Serves six.

## SMOKED SALMON AND POTATO SCALLOP

| | | |
|---|---|---|
| ¼ cup | (50 g) | butter or margarine |
| ½ cup | (1 dl) | minced onion |
| ¼ cup | (½ dl) | chopped green pepper |
| 1 tbsp | (1 tbsp) | flour |
| 1 tsp | (1 tsp) | salt |
| ¼ tsp | (¼ tsp) | pepper |
| 3 cups | (7 dl) | raw potatoes, cut in thin slices |
| 3 oz | (1½ hg) | smoked salmon, cut into ½″ (1 cm) pieces |
| 2 | (2) | eggs |
| 1¼ cups | (3 dl) | milk and cream, mixed |
| | | paprika |

Sauté onion in butter together with green pepper until wilted, 8–10 minutes, but make sure it does not brown. Remove from heat and mix in flour. Boil potatoes about 10 minutes and drain. In a greased baking dish put ⅓ of potatoes, a little pepper, then half of onion mixture and half of salmon. Continue with these layers, and the top layer will then be potatoes. Beat eggs with salt, milk and cream slightly and pour over mixture in baking dish. Sprinkle with paprika and bake in medium oven—350° F or 175° C—covered with foil for about 15 minutes, and without foil an additional 30 minutes. Serves six.

## SALMON AND MACARONI CASSEROLE

| | | |
|---|---|---|
| 1¼ cups | (3 dl) | elbow macaroni |
| 2 tbsp | (2 tbsp) | butter or margarine |
| ¼ cup | (½ dl) | minced onion |
| ¼ cup | (½ dl) | chopped green pepper |
| 2 tbsp | (2 tbsp) | flour |
| 1½ cups | (4 dl) | milk |
| | | salt and pepper |
| 1 can | (1 can) | whole kernel corn, drained (about 2 cups—5 dl) |
| 3 | (3) | hard boiled eggs, chopped |
| 1 tsp | (1 tsp) | Worcestershire sauce |
| ¼ lb | (2 hg) | smoked salmon |
| ¼ cup | (½ dl) | bread crumbs and a little butter or margarine |

Boil macaroni in salted water until tender and drain well. Melt butter or margarine, sauté onion and green pepper over low heat until wilted, but do not brown. Mix in flour and stir and add milk, a little bit at a time. Add salt and pepper. Stir in corn, eggs and Worcestershire sauce. In a greased baking dish, put macaroni mixed with the smoked salmon, cut up into bits of ½–¾″ (about 2 cm). Pour over sauce and sprinkle bread crumbs on top and dot with butter. Bake without cover in medium oven—350° F or 175° C—about 30 minutes. Serves six.

## SALMON LOAF ALASKA

| | | |
|---|---|---|
| 1 can (1 lb) | (1 can—½ kg) | canned salmon, or two smaller cans, or an equal amount of cold cooked salmon |
| 1¼ cups | (3 dl) | mashed potatoes |
| ¼ cup | (½ dl) | finely chopped celery |
| 1 tsp | (1 tsp) | minced onion |
| 1 tbsp | (1 tbsp) | freshly pressed lemon juice salt and pepper to taste |
| 2 tbsp | (2 tbsp) | mayonnaise |
| 1 | (1) | egg white |
| ¼ cup | (½ dl) | mayonnaise |

Drain salmon and remove skin and bones. Break up into rather large pieces and put into a large bowl. Mix together salmon and mashed potatoes, celery, onion, lemon juice and 2 tbsp mayonnaise. Add salt and pepper to taste. Pour mixture into a greased loaf pan (about 4 x 8"—10 x 20 cm). Beat egg white until stiff and mix with remaining mayonnaise and spread this on top of salmon mixture. Bake in medium oven—350° F or 175° C—30–35 minutes or until loaf is golden brown in color. Cut into slices and serve piping hot with a green salad. Serves 5–6.

## SEAFOOD CASSEROLE

| | | |
|---|---|---|
| 2 | (2) | eggs, slightly beaten |
| 1 cup | (2½ dl) | milk |
| 2 tbsp | (2 tbsp) | melted butter salt and pepper to taste |
| 1 tbsp | (1 tbsp) | freshly pressed lemon juice |
| ½ tsp | (½ tsp) | dry mustard |
| 1 cup, scant | (2 dl) | bread crumbs |
| 1½ cups | (4 dl) | lobster meat, crabmeat or shrimp (or a mixture of same) |

Blend eggs, milk and butter, add salt and pepper to taste and add dry mustard. Pour in bread crumbs and lemon juice and add shellfish, mixing well. Pour mixture into a greased baking dish and bake in medium oven—350° F or 175° C—about 40 minutes. Serve with melted butter and a fresh green salad, or cole slaw. Serves six.

## LOBSTER NEWBURG

*Lobster is not for every-day eating, but is strongly recommended for special occasions. These recipes were designed for the northern variety of lobster which has big claws. Rock lobster can be substituted in either dish so far as flavor is concerned, but it might be a problem to use its shell in Lobster Thermidor.*

| About 2 lbs | (1 kg) | boiled lobster |
|---|---|---|
| ¼ cup | (50 g) | butter or margarine |
| 1 tbsp | (1 tbsp) | flour |
| | | salt and paprika to taste |
| | | pinch of nutmeg |
| 1 cup | (2½ dl) | light cream |
| 3 | (3) | egg yolks |
| 2 tbsp | (2 tbsp) | sherry |

Take lobster meat out of shells and claws and cut into cubes. Melt butter, add flour and spices and stir vigorously, then add cream a little at a time. Bring to a boil and mix in lobster meat and when throughly warm, add the lightly beaten egg yolks and sherry. Let simmer until mixture thickens, but *it must not boil* as the eggs would then curdle. Serve with rice or on toast. For 4 people.

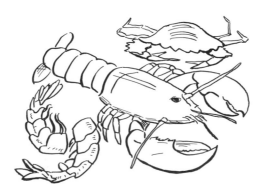

# LOBSTER THERMIDOR

| | | |
|---|---|---|
| 2 | (2) | boiled lobsters (about 1½ lbs or ¾ kg) each |
| 2 tbsp | (2 tbsp) | butter |
| 2 tbsp | (2 tbsp) | flour |
| 1 tsp | (1 tsp) | dry mustard |
| | | salt to taste and a pinch of cayenne |
| 1 tbsp | (1 tbsp) | minced parsley |
| 1 cup | (2½ dl) | light cream |
| ⅓ cup | (¾ dl) | white wine |
| ¼ cup | (½ dl) | grated Parmesan cheese |

Cut lobsters in halves lengthwise. Remove meat from shells and claws and cube it. Melt butter and let lobster meat sauté in this for about five minutes, add flour, spices and cream. Stir well and add wine and put mixture carefully back into lobster shells, sprinkle grated cheese on top and bake in hot oven—425° F or 220° C—about 10 minutes, or only brown them slightly under broiler. If desired, ¼ cup (½ dl) sliced mushrooms, sautéed in butter, may be added. Serves 4.


# POT ROAST IN FOIL

*This roast takes care of itself completely, once it has been put into the oven. It is therefore ideal if you want to go for a carefree hike on a Sunday morning, and return to find a dinner practically ready to be eaten.*

| | | |
|---|---|---|
| | | Pot roast of 4 or 5 lbs (2 kg) |
| 1 pkg | (1 pkg) | dehydrated onion soup mix, or one finely chopped onion |
| 1 can | (1 can) | cream of mushroom soup |
| ¼ cup | (½ dl) | red wine, if desired |
| | | salt and pepper |

Place the pot roast on a large piece of aluminum foil. Sprinkle the dry soup mixture on top, pour mushroom soup carefully over (also wine, if this is used) and close up foil carefully all around so that contents do not drain out during roasting. Roast in low-medium oven—325° F or 160° C—about 3 hours. After this time the roast is completely ready to be cut up and served, and the gravy is ready at the same time. Be careful, however, when you pour it out of the foil. Serves 6–8.

## BACHELORS' ROAST

|          |           | Pot roast of 4 or 5 lbs (2 kg) |
|----------|-----------|--------------------------------|
|          |           | salt and pepper to taste       |
| 3 tbsp   | (3 tbsp)  | butter or margarine            |
| 1        | (1)       | small bottle of Coca-Cola      |
| 1        | (1)       | small bottle of ketchup        |

Brown roast well on all sides in a dutch oven or a large frying pan. Place on aluminum foil in a baking dish, pour Coca-Cola and ketchup over, cover well with the foil, sealing all edges so that no liquid drains out during roasting. Roast in slow oven—325° F or 160° C—about 3 hours. Slice the meat and serve with gravy which has been formed during roasting. For 6 or 8 people.

## SAUERBRATEN

*This dish is one of the most popular German-American specialties, in spite of the time it takes to prepare it. You can use moderately tough meat, as the marinade will make it tender enough to "melt in your mouth".*

**Pot roast, 4–6 lbs. (2–3 kg)**

**Marinade:**

|          |           |                                        |
|----------|-----------|----------------------------------------|
| 8        | (8)       | whole cloves                           |
| 1 tsp    | (1 tsp)   | whole peppercorns                      |
| 2        | (2)       | bay leaves                             |
|          |           | pinch of thyme                         |
| 1        | (1)       | large onion, thinly sliced             |
| 2        | (2)       | cloves of garlic (may be omitted)      |
|          |           | salt                                   |
|          |           | vinegar and water, in equal amounts to cover. |

Place meat in an earthenware dish, pour marinade over, using sufficient vinegar and water to cover meat. Cover the dish and let stand for three or four days, turning the meat twice a day.

Thereafter, take meat out of marinade, dry it well and brown in butter or margarine. In the meantime, boil the marinade until liquid has been reduced to half, and add to the meat in a Dutch oven. Also add the following ingredients:

| | | |
|---|---|---|
| 1 | (1) | small can tomato paste (about ½ cup—1 dl) |
| 1 tbsp | (1 tbsp) | brown sugar |
| 1 tbsp | (1 tbsp) | freshly pressed lemon juice |
| 1 cup | (2½ dl) | red wine |
| 2-3 | (2-3) | strips of lemon peel |
| 6 | (6) | ginger snaps, crumbled |
| 1 tbsp | (1 tbsp) | Worcestershire sauce |

Let it all simmer over very low heat about 3½-4 hours or until meat is tender. Remove meat, keep it warm. Strain the gravy, pour some around meat and serve the rest in a bowl.

## BEEF STEW ORIENTAL

| | | |
|---|---|---|
| 2 lbs | (1 kg) | stewing beef |
| 2 tbsp | (2 tbsp) | butter or margarine |
| 1 tsp | (1 tsp) | chili powder |
| 1 tsp | (1 tsp) | ginger |
| 2 tsp | (2 tsp) | salt |
| | | a pinch of tumeric, if desired |
| 1 | (1) | medium onion, thinly sliced |
| 1 | (1) | clove of garlic (may be omitted) |
| 1 can | (1 can) | tomato paste (about ½ cup) |
| 1 tsp | (1 tsp) | curry |

Brown onion slightly in a little butter or margarine, sauté for a few minutes, then set aside. Cut meat in rather large cubes and work in spices (except curry) with hands, then brown meat. Add onion, tomato paste and about 1 cup (2 dl) water. Cover and let simmer over very low heat for about 1½ hours. Add curry just before serving. For 5 or 6 portions.

# CHOP SUEY

*This is one of the most popular dishes in Chinese restaurants in the United States. It is rumored that it would hardly be recognized in China. Whether this is true or not, it is good to eat and is wonderful to use when you have to make the most of some leftover meat.*

| | | |
|---|---|---|
| ½–1 lb | (¼–½ kg) | veal or pork, cut into small cubes |
| 1 | (1) | onion, thinly sliced |
| 1½ cups | (4 dl) | celery, thinly sliced |
| 1 | (1) | small paprika, chopped |
| ¾ cup | (1¾ dl) | raw rice |
| 5 cups | (12 dl) | bouillon (stock or made with cubes) |
| 1–2 tsp | (1–2 tsp) | salt |
| | | pinch of pepper |
| 1–2 tbsp | (1–2 tbsp) | soy sauce |

Brown meat in butter or margarine, then brown onion. Add the remaining ingredients and let it simmer for about 30 minutes covered, and an additional 10 minutes without cover. Serve piping hot in small bowls. For 5 or 6 people.

This dish can easily be made by using leftover meat, but lessen cooking time accordingly. Also, the rice may be cooked and served separately.

# NEW ENGLAND BOILED DINNER

| | | |
|---|---|---|
| 1 | (1) | smoked pork shoulder or ham, 4–6 lbs (2–3 kg) |
| 8 | (8) | carrots |
| 8 | (8) | small onions |
| 4–5 | (4–5) | potatoes, cut in large pieces |
| 2 | (2) | small turnips, cut in pieces |
| 1 | (1) | small head of cabbage |

If the meat is very salty, put it in cold water to soak for 6–8 hours. Drain and wipe well and put in a large kettle with cold water and bring to a boil. Skim. Let meat simmer under cover 3–3½ hours, or until it is tender. Remove meat and skim off extra grease which will float on top. Add carrots, onions, potatoes and turnips and bring to a boil, simmer for 20 minutes, then add cabbage, cut in 8 wedges and cook an additional 20–25 minutes, or until all vegetables are tender. Put meat back in kettle to get thoroughly warm, then place on a large platter with the vegetables nicely arranged around it. Serves 8.

## SWEET AND PUNGENT PORK

| | | |
|---|---|---|
| 1 lb | (½ kg) | lean pork, cut into 1″ (2 cm) cubes |
| 1 small can | (1 small can) | pineapple, cut into pieces (about 1 cup—2 dl) |
| 2 tbsp | (2 tbsp) | flour |
| 2 tbsp | (2 tbsp) | vinegar |
| 2 tbsp | (2 tbsp) | brown sugar |
| ¼ cup | (½ dl) | finely minced onion |
| ¼ cup | (½ dl) | finely chopped green pepper |
| 2 tbsp | (2 tbsp) | soy sauce |

If pork is fat enough, brown meat in its own fat, otherwise in a little butter or margarine. Remove from frying pan and brown onion and green pepper slightly, then return meat to pan. Drain juice from pineapple can and add sufficient water to make 1 cup (2½ dl) and pour over meat together with vinegar, brown sugar and soy sauce. Stir flour in a little water and add after about ten minutes, let it cook for an additional 5 minutes and add pineapple. Serve with rice. Makes 4-6 portions.

New England Boiled Dinner

# HAM A LA KING

*Ham is usually quite tasty, whether it is from the butcher's or from a can. But if you have one that is lacking in flavor, you can use these recipes to make it tasty and interesting. And if you are starting with a full-flavored ham, so much the better.*

| | | |
|---|---|---|
| 1 can | (1 can) | fully cooked ham—1 lb size (½ kg) |
| 2 tbsp | (2 tbsp) | butter or margarine |
| 3 tbsp | (3 tbsp) | flour |
| | | salt and pepper to taste |
| 1½ cups | (4 dl) | milk or milk and cream, mixed |
| ½ tsp | (½ tsp) | Worcestershire sauce |
| 1 cup, scant | (2 dl) | grated cheese (Swiss type) |
| 3 tbsp | (3 tbsp) | chopped sweet pickles, well drained |

Remove gelatin and unnecessary fat from ham and cut in small cubes. Melt butter in a heavy sauce pan, stir in flour and add milk, a little at a time. When brought to a boil and even in texture, add Worcestershire sauce and cheese, and stir until cheese is completely dissolved. Add ham and pickles, salt and pepper to taste and simmer over low heat until completely hot. Serve over a whole, boiled cauliflower, with rice or potatoes. Serves 4-6.

## HAM CASSEROLE STROGANOFF

| | | |
|---|---|---|
| ½ lb | (2 hg) | noodles |
| 4 tbsp | (4 tbsp) | butter or margarine |
| ½ cup | (1 dl) | finely minced onion |
| 1 | (1) | clove garlic, finely minced (may be omitted) |
| 1 can | (1 can) | mushrooms (6 oz–¼ l) |
| 1 can | (1 can) | fully cooked ham–1 lb (½ kg) |
| 1 tbsp | (1 tbsp) | flour |
| 1 can | (1 can) | tomato paste–4 oz (1 dl) |
| ¼ cup | (½ dl) | red wine |
| 1¼ cups | (3 dl) | bouillon |
| ¼ tsp | (¼ tsp) | pepper |
| 1 cup | (2 dl) | sour cream |
| ⅔ cup | (1½ dl) | grated Parmesan cheese |

Cook noodles in salted water about 10 minutes. Drain and run cool water over them so they will not stick together. Sauté onion, garlic and mushrooms in butter for about 5 minutes, but make sure it does not get too brown. Cut ham in cubes, (removing gelatin and unnecessary fat) and add to onion mixture, bring to a boil. Simmer an additional 5 minutes, add flour dissolved in a little cold water, tomato paste, red wine and bouillon. Add pepper and simmer about 10 minutes, stirring now and then. Remove from heat and mix in sour cream. In a baking dish, put one third of noodles, then one third of ham mixture and continue with these layers twice more. Sprinkle with grated cheese and bake in medium-warm oven–375° F or 190° C–about 25 minutes. Serves six.

## HAM SHISH KEBAB

| | | |
|---|---|---|
| 1 can | (1 can) | sliced pineapple |
| ½ cup, scant | (1 dl) | white wine |
| 1½ tsp | (1½ tsp) | ginger |
| 1 tbsp | (1 tbsp) | dry mustard |
| ½ tsp | (½ tsp) | salt |

| | | |
|---|---|---|
| 1 | (1) | **canned ham, about 2 lbs. (1 kg)** |
| 3 | (3) | **green peppers, cut in squares** |
| ½ lb | (¼ kg) | **small white onions, boiled about 10 minutes** |

Drain juice from pineapple can and pour into a bowl, add wine, ginger, mustard and salt and stir until well blended. Cut ham into cubes of about 1″ (2–3 cm) and put into marinade and let them stand in this at least two hours, or overnight. Remove ham cubes and put on skewers, alternately with green peppers, onions (well drained), pineapple (cut into pieces). Brush with marinade and grill for about 10 minutes, turning skewers over and brushing with more marinade off and on. Serve immediately with rice. Makes 6 servings.

## STUFFED PORK CHOPS

| | | |
|---|---|---|
| 4 | (4) | **pork chops, cut about 2″ (5 cm) thick with a "pocket" cut all the way to the bone in the middle** |
| | | **salt and pepper** |

**Stuffing:**

| | | |
|---|---|---|
| 2 tbsp | (2 tbsp) | **butter or margarine** |
| ½ cup | (1 dl) | **finely minced onion** |
| ½ cup | (1 dl) | **chopped celery** |
| 1½ cups | (4 dl) | **soft bread cubes (cut about 4 slices white bread in ½″ (1 cm) cubes** |
| ¼ cup | (½ dl) | **raisins** |
| 2 tbsp | (2 tbsp) | **minced parsley** |
| 1 tsp | (1 tsp) | **salt** |
| ½ tsp | (½ tsp) | **marjoram** |
| 1 | (1) | **apple, peeled and grated** |

Sauté onion and celery in butter in a frying pan until wilted, 8–10 minutes, but make sure it does not get too brown. Add bread cubes and brown slightly, remove from heat and add remaining ingredients and blend well. Fill "pockets" in pork chops with stuffing and stand preferably on a rack in a baking dish and pour about

½″ (1 cm) water in bottom of dish, but do not let water reach chops. Cover baking dish with its cover or aluminum foil and bake in medium oven—350° F or 175° C—45 minutes. Remove cover or foil and bake an additional 40–45 minutes, or until chops are tender and nicely brown in color. Serves 4.

## PORK CHOPS CREOLE

| | | |
|---|---|---|
| 6 | (6) | pork chops |
| 1 | (1) | medium onion, chopped |
| 2 tbsp | (2 tbsp) | green pepper, chopped |
| 1 can | (1 can) | tomato soup |
| 1 cup | (2 dl) | water |
| ¼ cup | (½ dl) | ketchup |
| ½ tsp | (½ tsp) | tabasco |
| | | salt and pepper to taste |
| ¼ cup | (½ dl) | raw rice |

Brown chops, add pepper and salt to taste. Remove from pan, brown onion and peppers slightly and pour over pork chops in a heavy sauce pan. Then add tomato soup, mixed with water and ketchup. Add remaining ingredients and let simmer on very low heat about 1 hour. If mixture should get too thick, add a little hot water during cooking. Serves 6.

## SHANGHAI PORK AND VEGETABLES

| | | |
|---|---|---|
| ½ lb | (¼ kg) | thin spaghetti |
| 6 tbsp | (6 tbsp) | salad oil |
| 2 | (2) | eggs, slightly beaten |
| ½ lb | (¼ kg) | lean pork, cut in thin strips |
| 3 tbsp | (3 tbsp) | soy sauce |
| 1 tsp | (1 tsp) | sugar |
| 1 lb | (½ kg) | Chinese cabbage, or white cabbage, cut in thin strips or shredded |
| ½ cup | (1 dl) | fresh or canned mushrooms, sliced thin |
| 2 tbsp | (2 tbsp) | water |
| ½ tsp | (½ tsp) | salt |

Boil spaghetti in salted water until tender and rinse in cold water. Mix 2 tbsp. of salad oil with the cold spaghetti. Heat 1 tbsp salad oil in a frying pan and pour in the slightly beaten eggs so that they form a large pancake. Do not stir but fry over low heat until congealed. Cool and cut it into thin strips. Heat up another 1 tbsp. salad oil in frying pan and add pork and stir and let it cook slowly for about 2 minutes or until all pieces of pork have turned white in color. Mix in soy-sauce, sugar, cabbage, mushrooms and water. Cover and bring to boil, turn down heat and let it simmer for about 10 minutes. Heat 2 tbsp. salad oil in another frying pan (or heavy saucepan) and spread spaghetti evenly in this and cook about 2 minutes, stir and cook another 2 minutes. Add salt and pour into other pan and mix everything together. Serves 4-5.

## TEXAS BARBECUED SPARERIBS

*Spareribs, with a biting barbecue sauce, is one of the favorites of American men. The meat may be cooked on an outside grill, but it has to be watched carefully there, as it burns easily.*

| | | |
|---|---|---|
| 3 lbs | (1½ kg) | spareribs |

**Texas Barbecue Sauce:**

| | | |
|---|---|---|
| 1 cup | (2½ dl) | ketchup |
| ¼ cup | (½ dl) | vinegar |
| 2 tbsp | (2 tbsp) | Worcestershire sauce |
| 1 tsp | (1 tsp) | salt |
| ½ tsp | (½ tsp) | pepper |
| 2 tsp | (2 tsp) | chili powder |
| 1–2 | (1–2) | medium onions, finely minced |
| 1½ cups | (4 dl) | water |

Wipe spareribs with damp cloth and place in a roasting pan. Mix together all ingredients for barbecue sauce, stir until well blended and pour on top of meat. Cover and bake in medium oven—350° F or 175° C—about 1½ hour. During the last 30 minutes, uncover. The meat should be turned and basted with barbecue sauce several times during baking. Serves 5-6.

## CHINESE BARBECUED SPARERIBS

| 3 lbs | (1½ kg) | spareribs |
|---|---|---|

**Barbecue Sauce:**

| ½ cup | (1 dl) | soy sauce |
|---|---|---|
| ½ cup | (1 dl) | pineapple juice |
| 2 tbsp | (2 tbsp) | sherry |
| 1 | (1) | clove garlic, crushed |
| 1 | (1) | medium onion, finely minced |
| 1 tsp | (1 tsp) | ginger |
| 3 tbsp | (3 tbsp) | brown sugar |

Mix together all ingredients for sauce and pour over spareribs. Marinate for several hours, or preferably over-night, in refrigerator. Turn spareribs two or three times. Broil spareribs about 6″ (15 cm) from heat, 20–30 minutes on each side, or until they are tender and well browned. Baste frequently with sauce during broiling. Serves 6–8. This dish can also be baked in the oven in the same manner as described in the previous recipe.

## VEAL FILLET SCALLOPINI

| | | |
|---|---|---|
| ¼ cup | (50 g) | butter or margarine |
| 1 cup | (2½ dl) | minced onion |
| 1 can | (1 can) | mushrooms, about 1 cup (2½ dl), or same quantity cooked fresh mushrooms |
| 1½ tsp | (1½ tsp) | salt |
| | | pepper |
| 1 cup | (2½ dl) | sour cream |
| 1½ lbs | (¾ kg) | veal fillets, cut very thin |
| 3 tbsp | (3 tbsp) | flour |
| 1 cup | (2 dl) | dry white wine |
| | | chopped parsley |

Sauté onion and mushrooms in 3 tbsp. butter over low heat for about 10 minutes until tender. Add salt and pepper and 3 tbsp sour cream and mix well. Put 1 tbsp. of this mixture on one end of each fillet, roll it together and fasten with toothpick. Roll fillets in flour and brown in remaining butter. Pour wine over them, bring to a boil, then turn down heat and let simmer under cover 30–35 minutes, or until meat is tender. Remove meat and put on hot platter, remove toothpicks. Mix remaining flour with 1 tbsp. water and add to frying pan, mixing well, and let boil for a few minutes. Remove from heat and add remaining sour cream. Let mixture get hot, but do *not boil,* and pour over meat. Garnish with fresh chopped parsley. Serves 4–5.

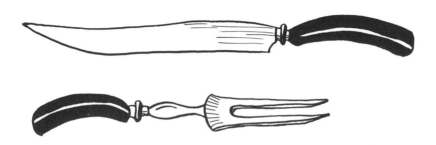

# VITELLO TONNATO

*This dish is a good choice for summer days when you have a lot of company. It can be prepared completely in advance, and as it may be served with potato or green bean salad which can also be fixed beforehand, you have only to sit down and enjoy the meal when it is time to eat. That is, if others will set the table.*

| | | |
|---|---|---|
| 2–3 lbs | (1½ kg) | veal roast, rolled, or from the leg, boneless |
| 1 can | (1 can) | tuna |
| 1 | (1) | medium onion, finely minced |
| 8 | (8) | anchovy fillets, finely chopped |
| 2 cups | (5 dl) | dry white wine |
| ⅓ cup | (¾ dl) | olive oil |
| | | juice from 2 lemons |
| 2 tbsp | (2 tbsp) | pickles, chopped |
| | | salt and pepper |

The meat should be tied so that it will keep its shape during cooking. Place it in a heavy saucepan together with broken-up tuna, onion, anchovies, salt, pepper and wine. Cover and bring to a boil. Skim and let simmer over very low heat about 1 hour and 45 minutes. Remove meat and put in a big bowl. Pass everything from the pot through a sieve, or purée it in a blender. Add olive oil, lemon juice and chopped pickles and stir well. Pour over meat and keep in refrigerator for 2 days. Serve meat at room temperature, cut in very thin slices and serve together with the marinade which first should be well blended. Garnish with lemon wedges and parsley. Serves 5–6.

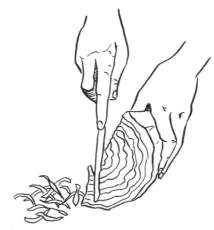

## LAMB CURRY

| | | |
|---|---|---|
| 2 tbsp | (2 tbsp) | butter or margarine |
| ¼ cup | (½ dl) | finely minced onion |
| 2 tbsp | (2 tbsp) | raisins |
| 2 tbsp | (2 tbsp) | shredded coconut |
| | | salt and pepper to taste |
| 2 tbsp | (2 tbsp) | freshly pressed lemon juice |
| 1 tsp | (1 tsp) | curry |
| 1½–2 cups | (4–5 dl) | cooked lamb, cut in large cubes |
| 1 cup | (2½ dl) | leftover gravy, *or* |
| 1 cup | (2½ dl) | bouillon, mixed with 1 tbsp flour |

Sauté onion lightly in butter or margarine, add curry and meat. Stir in raisins, shredded coconut and add pepper and salt to taste. Simmer for about 20 minutes. Just before serving, add lemon juice. Serve with boiled rice. 4–5 portions.

## STEAK AND KIDNEY PIE

| | | |
|---|---|---|
| 2 lbs | (1 kg) | rump steak |
| ½ lb | (¼ kg) | veal kidneys |
| 2 tbsp | (2 tbsp) | butter or margarine |
| | | salt and pepper to taste |
| 1 | (1) | small onion, finely minced |
| | | chopped parsley |
| | | crust for single pie, see page 41 |

Cut beef in small strips, brown in butter, add salt and pepper to taste. Remove fat and membranes from the kidneys and cut into thin slices and brown in butter, then brown onion. In a shallow casserole make alternate layers of beef and kidney, sprinkling each layer with onion and parsley. Rinse out frying pan with a little water and pour over meat. Make a single pie crust and roll out on floured board. Wet edges of casserole and put pie crust on top, fitting it over the filling and pressing it down well at the edges to seal the dish. Cut some gashes in the top to allow steam to escape. Bake in medium oven—350° F or 175° C—1½–2 hours or until meat is tender. Serve direct from casserole. Serves 5–6.

## BARBECUED FRANKFURTERS WITH BACON

| 12 | (12) | frankfurters |
|----|------|--------------|
| 2 | (2) | slices of broiled or fried bacon |

Barbecue sauce:

| 1 tbsp | (1 tbsp) | butter |
|--------|----------|--------|
| ½ | (½) | medium onion, finely chopped |
| ½ tsp | (½ tsp) | pepper |
| 1 tbsp | (1 tbsp) | sugar |
| 1 tsp | (1 tsp) | dry mustard |
| 1 tsp | (1 tsp) | paprika |
| ½ cup | (1¼ dl) | ketchup |
| ⅓ cup | (¾ dl) | water |
| 4 tsp | (4 tsp) | Worcestershire sauce |

Sauté onion in butter over low heat until tender, but do not let it get brown. Add the remaining ingredients for sauce and bring to a boil, stirring now and then. Remove from heat. With a sharp knife, cut a 4″ (10 cm) slit along each frankfurter and place in a greased baking dish with the cut side up. Pour over sauce and bake in medium oven—350° F or 175° C—about 25 minutes and baste with sauce once or twice during baking. Put bacon slices on top and serve. For 6 people.

## STUFFED FRANKS

| 8 | (8) | frankfurters |
|---|-----|--------------|
| | | mustard |
| 2 cups | (5 dl) | mashed potatoes |
| ¼ cup | (½ dl) | onion, finely minced |
| 1 to 2 tbsp | (1 to 2 tbsp) | chopped pimiento, or fresh red pepper |
| ¼ cup | (½ dl) | chopped parsley |

Pour boiling water over frankfurters and let them stand 8–10 minutes. Cut a slit lengthwise of each frankfurter and spread mustard in this. Mix the remaining ingredients well and stuff mixture into and on top of frankfurters. Bake in medium oven—350° F or 175° C—10-15 minutes. Serves 6-8.

# HAMBURGERS

*Hamburgers are among the most popular and easily prepared foods in American homes and restaurants, and are often cooked on an outdoor grill. They are particularly liked by children, some of whom would eat almost nothing else if given free choice. During the preparation of this book, I served my family with unusually good and varied meals, as tests of the various recipes followed each other closely. But after a while my 9-year old boy asked complainingly, "Do we have to eat recipes all the time? Can't we ever have just hamburgers?"*

> **1 lb (½ kg)    chopped beef, neither very fat nor very lean (chopped chuck steak is good)
> salt and pepper**

For a real hamburger sandwich a good chopped beef is used without anything added. Shape meat lightly into 4-6 hamburgers and broil them on both sides either in the oven or on an outside grill, or fry them. You can start them with a little fat, or on a dry pan sprinkled with salt. Most people prefer them medium rare.

Different things can be added to the chopped meat according to taste, such as minced onion, egg, bread crumbs, etc.

The hamburgers are served in slit and warmed buns (hamburger or barbecue rolls), plain or with ketchup, pickles or a slice of raw onion.

## CHEESEBURGERS

These are prepared in the same manner as hamburgers except a slice of cheese is added on top after turning. It should be broiled until almost melted before the top part of the bun is put on.

## HAMBURGER CHEESE CASSEROLE

| | | |
|---|---|---|
| 1 lb | (½ kg) | ground beef |
| ½ cup | (1 dl) | bread crumbs |
| 1 | (1) | egg |
| 1 | (1) | medium onion, finely minced |
| | | salt and pepper to taste |
| ½ cup | (1 dl) | water |
| | | cheese slices |
| 1 can | (1 can) | tomato sauce or soup (about 1 cup (2½ dl) |

Blend ground beef with bread crumbs, egg, onion, water and add salt and pepper to taste. Form 8–9 small hamburgers, rather thick. Slice these in half and put a slice of cheese between the two halves. Place in a greased baking dish, pour tomato sauce or soup over them and bake in medium oven—350° F or 175° C—40-45 minutes. The cheese should then be completely melted and mixed with sauce. Serve with mashed potatoes, boiled rice or noodles to 5-6 people.

## HAMBURGER PINWHEELS

| | | |
|---|---|---|
| 3 tbsp | (3 tbsp) | minced onion |
| 1 tbsp | (1 tbsp) | butter or margarine |
| ½ cup | (1 dl) | bread crumbs |
| ⅓ cup | (¾ dl) | milk |
| ¾ lb | (3 hg) | chopped beef |
| | | salt and pepper to taste |

**For dough:**

| | | |
|---|---|---|
| 1½ cups | (4 dl) | flour |
| 1 tsp | (1 tsp) | salt |
| 2 tsp | (2 tsp) | baking powder |
| ½ cup | (110 g) | butter or margarine |
| ¾ cup | (1¾ dl) | milk |

Sauté onion in butter or margarine until tender, but do not brown. Mix together with chopped meat, salt and pepper, bread crumbs and milk and blend well. Sift together flour, baking powder and salt. Cut in shortening with pastry cutter or two knives until mixture is crumbly. Add milk, a little at a time, until a soft dough has been formed. Put on floured board and knead 15 seconds. Roll into a 9 x 12″ (23 x 30 cm) rectangle. Spread with meat mixture and roll together lengthwise, wetting edge to seal. Cut in slices ½-¾″ (1-1½ cm) thick and put on a greased baking plate. Bake in hot oven—400° F or 200° C—about 25 minutes. 4-5 servings.

## HAM LOAF SUPREME

| | | |
|---|---|---|
| ¾ lb | (3 hg) | cooked ham |
| ½ lb | (¼ kg) | ground veal |
| ¼ lb | (1½ hg) | ground pork |
| 2 | (2) | eggs, slightly beaten |
| ¾ cup | (2 dl) | bread crumbs |
| ¾ cup | (2 dl) | milk |
| | | pinch of pepper |
| 2 tsp | (2 tsp) | dry mustard |
| ¼ cup | (½ dl) | brown sugar |
| ⅓ cup | (¾ dl) | pineapple juice |

Mix together the different kinds of meat, add eggs, bread crumbs, milk and pepper, and blend well. Pour mixture into a greased loaf pan. Spread on top of loaf, a mixture of mustard and brown sugar and pour pineapple juice over. Bake in medium oven—350° F or 175° C—about 1½ hours. Serves 5-6.

Ham Loaf Supreme, Potatoes Charlotte, peas, Waldorf Salad

# STUFFED PEPPERS

| | | |
|---|---|---|
| 6–8 | (6–8) | green peppers (depending on size) |
| ⅔ cup | (1½ dl) | raw rice (or twice the quantity of cooked rice) |
| 1 cup | (2½ dl) | water |
| 1 lb | (½ kg) | chopped meat |
| 1 | (1) | egg |
| 1 can | (1 can) | tomato paste—about 4 oz (1 dl) |
| | | salt and pepper to taste |

Boil rice in salted water until almost tender, let cool and blend with chopped meat, egg and half of tomato paste. Add salt and pepper to taste. Cut green peppers lengthwise and cut away white membranes and seeds. Fill pepper halves with meat mixture and spread the remaining tomato paste on top. Put in a greased baking dish and bake in medium oven—350° F or 175° C—50–60 minutes. Should peppers dry out too much during baking, add a little hot water to baking dish. Serves 5–6.

# CHEESEBURGER LOAF

| | | |
|---|---|---|
| 1 lb | (½ kg) | chopped meat |
| ½ cup | (1 dl) | milk |
| 1 | (1) | medium onion, finely minced |
| 1 | (1) | egg |
| ¾ cup | (2 dl) | bread crumbs |
| 1½ tsp | (1½ tsp) | salt |
| 1 tsp | (1 tsp) | dry mustard |
| 1 tbsp | (1 tbsp) | ketchup |
| ¾ cup | (2 dl) | grated cheese, preferably Cheddar type |

Mix together all ingredients except cheese. Cover a loaf pan with aluminum foil, sprinkle half the cheese evenly on bottom and add half of meat mixture. Add remaining cheese and then the rest of the meat mixture and bake in medium oven—350° F or 175° C—1 hour. Let loaf stand for about 10 minutes before it is turned over onto a serving platter and foil is removed. Garnish with tomato slices and parsley. Serves 5–6.

# SWEDISH MEAT BALLS

*Spaghetti with meat balls is probably the most popular of the gifts the American kitchen has received from Italy. But the original meat ball recipes are often replaced by an almost-Swedish variety, which makes a good combination with spaghetti and sauce, and are excellent by themselves both as a main meat dish and as party snacks served on toothpicks.*

| | | |
|---|---|---|
| 1 lb | (½ kg) | **chopped meat (preferably a mixture of ½ beef and ¼ each of pork and veal)** |
| 3 tbsp | (3 tbsp) | **finely minced onions** |
| 2 tbsp | (2 tbsp) | **butter** |
| ½ cup | (1½ dl) | **bread crumbs** |
| ¾ cup | (2 dl) | **milk** |
| 1 | (1) | **egg** |
| | | **salt and pepper to taste** |
| | | **pinch of ground allspice** |

Sauté onions in butter until golden brown. Soak bread crumbs in milk, then add ground meat, onions, egg and seasonings. Mix until smooth. For main meal use, shape meat balls with hands about 1½″ (3 cm) in diameter and brown in more butter on all sides. Shake pan continuously to keep round shape of meat balls. If used with spaghetti sauce, add meat balls to sauce and cook for about 10–15 minutes. If used by themselves, sauté meat balls in frying pan the same amount of time, then remove them and add a little water to pan to get all pan juice out, which is served with meat balls. For "smorgasbord" or for serving on tooth picks with cocktails, shape into very small balls, ¾″ (2 cm) in diameter and proceed in the same manner as described for larger meat balls.

## SPAGHETTI SAUCE

| | | |
|---|---|---|
| 1 tbsp | (1 tbsp) | bacon grease |
| ½ cup | (1 dl) | onion, minced |
| 1 | (1) | clove garlic, crushed (may be omitted) |
| 1 can | (1 can) | tomatoes (3 cups—8 dl) or 8–10 fresh tomatoes, peeled |
| 1 can | (1 can) | tomato paste—4 oz. (about 1 dl) |
| 1 tsp | (1 tsp) | oregano |
| 1 tsp | (1 tsp) | minced parsley |
| 2 tbsp | (2 tbsp) | sugar |

Sauté onion in bacon grease together with garlic, if this is used, until wilted. Add the remaining ingredients and bring to a boil, turn down heat as low as possible and let the sauce simmer very slowly at least four hours. 6–8 servings.

## QUICK SPAGHETTI SAUCE

| | | |
|---|---|---|
| 3 | (3) | slices bacon |
| 1 | (1) | onion, minced (about ⅓ cup—¾ dl) |
| 1 tbsp | (1 tbsp) | sugar |
| 1 tsp | (1 tsp) | oregano |
| 1 tsp | (1 tsp) | minced parsley |
| 1 can | (1 can) | tomato soup |
| ⅔ cup | (1½ dl) | water |

Spaghetti with meat balls and sauce

Fry bacon until crisp, set aside. Pour off excess fat but use a little to sauté onion until wilted. Add the remaining ingredients and simmer for about ½ hour. Just before serving, add crumbled bacon to sauce. Serves 5–6.

## MEXICAN MEAT BALLS WITH CHILI SAUCE

| | | |
|---|---|---|
| 1 lb | (½ kg) | chopped meat |
| ½ cup | (1 dl) | bread crumbs |
| ¼ cup | (½ dl) | milk |
| 1 | (1) | egg, slightly beaten |
| | | salt and pepper to taste |
| ½ tsp | (½ tsp) | oregano |
| 1 tsp | (1 tsp) | chili powder |

Mix together the above ingredients until well blended and make small meat balls. Brown in butter or margarine. Set aside.

**Chili Sauce:**

| | | |
|---|---|---|
| 1 tbsp | (1 tbsp) | salad oil |
| ½ cup | (1 dl) | finely minced onion |
| 1 | (1) | clove garlic, crushed (may be omitted) |
| ¼ tsp | (¼ tsp) | cumin, ground |
| 1 can | (1 can) | tomato paste—4 oz. (about 1 dl) |
| ½ cup | (1 dl) | ketchup |
| ¼ cup | (½ dl) | brown sugar |
| 1½ tbsp | (1½ tbsp) | chili powder |
| 1 tsp | (1 tsp) | salt |
| ¼ tsp | (¼ tsp) | oregano |

Sauté onion in salad oil together with garlic if this is used. Add remaining ingredients, turn down heat and let simmer for about 15 minutes. Add ¾ cup (2 dl) water and bring to a boil. Add the browned meat balls and let them simmer in sauce 20–25 minutes. Serve with rice or squares of corn bread (see page 7). Serves 5–6.

## RATATOUILLE

| | | |
|---|---|---|
| 2 | (2) | medium green peppers, cut into pieces |
| 2 | (2) | medium onions, cut into thin slices |
| 2 | (2) | zucchini squash, or cucumbers, cut into thick slices or pieces |
| 1 | (1) | egg plant, cut into cubes |
| 1 | (1) | clove garlic (may be omitted) |
| ¼ cup | (½ dl) | salad oil |
| 1 lb | (½ kg) | chopped meat |
| | | salt and pepper to taste |
| 4 | (4) | medium tomatoes, cut into wedges |
| 2 tbsp | (2 tbsp) | minced parsley |

Heat oil in frying pan and sauté onion, pepper and garlic (if such is used) for about 5 minutes. Remove from frying pan and brown chopped meat and break up with a fork so that a crumbly mixture forms. Put back onion mixture and add the remaining ingredients except parsley and let it simmer until all vegetables are tender. Add parsley and serve over boiled white rice. 5–6 servings.

## NOODLE AND PORK CASSEROLE

| | | |
|---|---|---|
| 8 oz | (3 hg) | noodles |
| 4 tbsp | (4 tbsp) | butter or margarine |
| 1 | (1) | medium onion, finely minced |
| 1 lb | (½ kg) | ground pork |
| ½ cup | (1 dl) | bread crumbs |
| ¼ cup | (½ dl) | milk |
| 1 tsp | (1 tsp) | cumin |
| 1 tsp | (1 tsp) | paprika |
| ¼ cup | (½ dl) | finely minced parsley |
| 3 | (3) | eggs, slightly beaten |
| ⅔ cup | (1½ dl) | milk and cream, mixed |
| ¼ cup | (½ dl) | grated cheese, Swiss type |
| | | salt and pepper to taste |

Boil noodles in salted water until *almost* tender. Sauté onion in 2 tbsp. butter in a frying pan for a few minutes, add ground pork and break up with a fork, and simmer, stirring and breaking up into smaller pieces until the pink color has disappeared from the meat. Mix milk with bread crumbs and add together with cumin, paprika and parsley. Add salt and pepper to taste. Put one layer of noodles in a greased baking dish, then a layer of meat mixture and continue until it is all used up. Top layer should be of noodles. Mix the slightly beaten eggs with milk, cream and cheese. Pour over contents in baking dish. Dot with remaining butter and bake in medium oven—350° F or 175° C—40-45 minutes. Serves 6-7.

## MACARONI CASSEROLE

| | | |
|---|---|---|
| 1 cup | (2½ dl) | elbow macaroni |
| | | salted water |
| ½ lb | (3 hg) | chopped meat |
| 1 tbsp | (1 tbsp) | butter or margarine |
| | | Quick Spaghetti Sauce (see page 78) |
| | | grated cheese |

Cook macaroni in salted water 10 minutes. Drain and rinse with cold water and drain well again. Melt butter or margarine in frying pan, add chopped meat and brown, breaking apart with a fork to make it crumbly. Mix macaroni, meat and spaghetti sauce, blend well and pour into greased baking dish, sprinkle with grated cheese and bake in medium oven—350° F or 175° C—20 minutes. Serves 4-5.

## MEXICALE SPAGHETTI BAKE

| | | |
|---|---|---|
| ½ lb | (¼ kg) | spaghetti or noodles |
| ¼ cup | (½ dl) | salad oil |
| 1 lb | (½ kg) | chopped meat |
| 1 | (1) | large onion, minced |
| 1 | (1) | green pepper, chopped |
| 1 | (1) | clove garlic, minced |
| 1 can | (1 can) | tomatoes—about 2 cups (6 dl) or 8–10 fresh tomatoes |
| 1 can | (1) | whole kernel corn (about 2 cups—5 dl) |
| 1 tsp | (1) | salt |
| ½ tsp | (½ tsp) | pepper |
| 2 tsp | (2 tsp) | chili powder |
| 1 tsp | (1 tsp) | Worcestershire sauce |
| ⅔ cup | (1½ dl) | black olives, sliced |

Boil spaghetti in salted water and drain. Rinse in cold water and drain well again. Brown chopped meat in oil, add onion, green pepper, garlic and continue to brown, breaking up chopped meat with a fork to make it crumbly. Add the remaining ingredients and mix well. Pour into a greased baking dish, cover and bake in medium oven—350° F or 175° C—about 1 hour. Serves 8.

## CALIFORNIA CASSEROLE

| | | |
|---|---|---|
| 1 lb | (½ kg) | chopped meat |
| 1 tbsp | (1 tbsp) | butter or margarine |
| 1 | (1) | large onion, finely minced |
| 1 | (1) | green pepper, chopped |
| 1 tbsp | (1 tbsp) | chili powder |
| 1 tbsp | (1 tbsp) | Worcestershire sauce |
| 1 can | (1 can) | tomatoes (2 cups—5 dl) or 6–8 fresh tomatoes |
| 2 cups | (5 dl) | cooked kidney beans (or canned) |
| ¾ cup | (2 dl) | rice, raw |
| ¼ cup | (½ dl) | green olives, chopped |
| ⅔ cup | (1½ dl) | grated cheese, Cheddar type |
| | | salt and pepper to taste |

Brown meat in butter or margarine, add onion, paprika, chili powder and salt and pepper to taste. Break up with a fork to make a crumbly mixture. Simmer about 5 minutes. Add Worcestershire sauce, tomatoes, beans and rice. Pour mixture in a greased baking dish and bake in medium oven—350° F or 175° C—45 minutes. Remove dish from oven, sprinkle chopped olives and cheese on top and bake an additional 15 minutes, or until cheese is completely melted. Serves 8.

## CHILI CON CARNE

| | | |
|---|---|---|
| 1½ cups | (4 dl) | kidney beans, or other brown beans |
| | | salt to taste |
| 1 | (1) | medium onion, minced |
| 1 tbsp | (1 tbsp) | butter or margarine |
| 1 lb | (½ kg) | chopped meat |
| | | salt and pepper to taste |
| 1 can | (1 can) | tomatoes—about 3 cups (8–10 dl) or 8–10 |
| | | fresh tomatoes) |
| 2 tbsp | (2 tbsp) | chili powder |

Rinse beans and soak for a few hours in cold water. Boil them in lightly salted water over low heat until beans are a little more than half tender (about 1–1½ hours, depending on the beans). Sauté onion in butter in frying pan for a few minutes and remove, then brown chopped meat, breaking up with a fork into crumbs. Pour chopped meat in heavy saucepan with beans, add onion, tomatoes and chili powder and simmer over low heat for 1 hour. Do not stir vigorously as the beans might get crushed. When beans are tender, taste mixture and add more chili powder if necessary. The dish should be very spicy—and really heat your throat. Serve immediately by itself or over boiled rice. For 6 people.

# COLUMBUS CASSEROLE

| | | |
|---|---|---|
| 1 cup | (2½ dl) | elbow macaroni |
| 4 | (4) | slices bacon |
| 1 lb | (½ kg) | beef liver, cubed |
| 3 tbsp | (3 tbsp) | flour |
| 1 tsp | (1 tsp) | salt |
| | | pepper to taste |
| ½ cup | (1 dl) | chopped onion |
| 1 can | (1 can) | mushroom soup |
| 1 cup | (2 dl) | milk |
| 1 tbsp | (1 tbsp) | soy sauce |
| 1 cup | (2½ dl) | whole kernel corn, canned |
| | | parsley |

Boil macaroni in salted water 10 minutes and drain. Rinse with cold water and drain again. Fry bacon slices lightly and set aside. Roll liver cubes in a mixture of salt and flour and brown in bacon grease. Remove from pan. Brown onion and sauté for a few minutes, put liver back in pan and simmer with onion about 15 minutes. Pour mushroom soup in a rather large baking dish, stir in milk and soy sauce, add macaroni and liver mixture, then corn, and mix well. Place bacon slices on top and bake in medium oven—350° F or 175° C—40 minutes. Just before serving sprinkle minced parsley on top. Serves 5.

## LIVER WITH CABBAGE ORIENTAL STYLE

| | | |
|---|---|---|
| 2 tbsp | (2 tbsp) | butter or margarine |
| 1 | (1) | medium onion, finely minced |
| 1 | (1) | small head of cabbage, shredded (about 6 cups—1½ liters) |
| 1 lb | (4 hg) | beef liver |
| 2 tbsp | (2 tbsp) | flour |
| 1 cup | (2 dl) | water |
| 1 tbsp | (1 tbsp) | soy sauce |
| | | salt and pepper to taste |

Brown onion lightly in butter or margarine, add cabbage and brown lightly and simmer for about 10 minutes. Cut liver into small cubes, roll in flour and brown in butter or margarine, add water and salt and pepper to taste and simmer for 5 minutes. Mix together cabbage, onion and liver and simmer an additional 5 minutes. Add soy sauce and serve immediately with rice. For 5-6 people.

# ROAST TURKEY

*For holiday dinners turkey is the number one favorite. It is almost always stuffed, both the stomach and neck opening. The stuffing, also called dressing, is usually delicious and it makes the meat more moist and tasty. Good stuffing can also be made with rice, and in a variety of ways, but this bread stuffing is the most popular.*

*Chicken may be stuffed and roasted in the same manner as turkey, but allowance must of course be made for its smaller stuffing capacity and for shorter cooking time.*

| | | |
|---|---|---|
| 1 | (1) | turkey, 10–13 lbs (5–6 kg) |
| | | stuffing (see following recipe which is about the right amount for a turkey of this size) |
| ½ cup | (1 dl) | salad oil |
| | | pepper and salt |

Check skin of turkey and with a pair of tweezers remove feather pockets which might remain. Stuff neck opening and stomach with the stuffing and fasten together by sewing with heavy cotton yarn or with skewers. Brush turkey with salad oil and bake in roasting pan in slow oven—325° F or 160° C. Place turkey on its side and let it remain like this ¼ of baking time, then move over to other side for same amount of time, then move onto stomach the same amount of time and for the remaining ¼ time place it on its back with the breast up. If surface should get too brown towards the end of baking time, place a cloth, soaked in salad oil, over turkey. When turkey is baked, remove yarn or skewers and scoop out stuffing carefully from turkey at the same time it is carved. Make gravy out of pan drippings. Below are baking times for turkeys of different weights in a—325° F or 160° C—oven:

| | | |
|---|---|---|
| 4–6 lbs | (2–3 kg) | 2–3 hours |
| 6–8 lbs | (3–4 kg) | 3–4 hours |
| 8–10 lbs | (4–5 kg) | 4–5 hours |
| 12–16 lbs | (6–8 kg) | 5–6 hours |
| 16–20 lbs | (8–10 kg) | 6–6½ hours |
| 20–24 lbs | (10–12 kg) | 6½–8 hours |

Holiday Turkey Dinner

## TURKEY STUFFING

| | | |
|---|---|---|
| 6–8 cups | (1½–2 l) | day old white bread, cut into cubes |
| 1 tbsp | (1 tbsp) | salt |
| ¼ tsp | (¼ tsp) | pepper |
| 2 tbsp | (2 tbsp) | thyme |
| ⅔ cup | (1½ dl) | minced onion |
| ½–¾ cup | (110–150 g) | melted butter or margarine |
| 1 cup | (2 dl) | chicken bouillon or hot water |
| 1 | (1) | egg, slightly beaten |

Mix together bread and spices. Sauté onion in 2 tbsp butter for about 5 minutes and add to bread mixture. Add liquid and blend thoroughly, add remaining butter and egg. Kidneys, liver, heart and gizzard can be cooked for about 1 hour, then chopped and mixed with stuffing. In such a case, the broth of this may be used instead of chicken bouillon or water. This stuffing is sufficient for a turkey of about 10–13 lbs. (5–6 kg).

## OVEN FRIED CHICKEN

| 1 | (1) | chicken, 2–3 lbs (1–1½ kg), cut into pieces |
| ¼ cup | (½ dl) | minced onion |
| 2 tbsp | (2 tbsp) | butter or margarine |
| | | salt and pepper to taste |
| | | paprika to taste |

Brown onion slightly in butter or margarine, set aside. Brown chicken well, add salt and pepper to taste and sprinkle with paprika. Place chicken in a greased baking dish, sprinkle onion on top and bake in medium oven—350° F or 175° C—about 50 minutes. Make a gravy of drippings and keep chicken warm in the meantime. Serve immediately. For 4 people.

## BAKED CHICKEN

| 1 | (1) | broiler-chicken (2–3 lbs (1–1½ kg) |

Cut up chicken in serving pieces and brown well in a little butter in frying pan. Place in greased baking dish and pour over it either one of the following sauces:

**Chicken with Sour Cream Sauce:**

| ½ cup | (1¼ dl) | sour cream |
| 1 cup | (3 dl) | onion soup (see recipe page 98) or canned onion soup |

Mix together these ingredients and pour over chicken. Bake in medium oven—350° F or 175° C—45–50 minutes. Serve on toast. 4–5 servings.

**Chicken Tchakhokkbell:**

| | | |
|---|---|---|
| 2 | (2) | medium onions, minced and sautéed in 2 tbsp. butter or margarine |
| ⅓ cup | (¾ dl) | sherry |
| ⅓ cup | (¾ dl) | tomato soup |
| | | salt, pepper and paprika to taste |

Mix together the ingredients for the sauce and pour over chicken in a baking dish and bake in medium oven—350° F or 175° C—about 1 hour. Serve with rice. 4–5 portions.

## CHICKEN ALOHA

*This chicken dish has its origin in Hawaii, and it really gives an exotic touch to a dinner. Serve it with boiled rice and some salad that includes pineapple, and you may almost hear the waves of the Pacific and the wind through palm trees.*

| | | |
|---|---|---|
| 1 | (1) | chicken, 2–3 lbs (1–1½ kg) |
| ½ cup | (1 dl) | soy sauce |
| 3 tbsp | (3 tbsp) | salad oil |
| 1½ tsp | (1½ tsp) | dry mustard |
| 1 tsp | (1 tsp) | ground ginger |
| ½ tsp | (½ tsp) | pepper |
| 1 | (1) | clove garlic, crushed |

Cut chicken in serving pieces. Mix together remaining ingredients and blend well. Marinate chicken in this and let stand at least 24 hours, turn over pieces now and then to make sure all get soaked by marinade. Place chicken in a greased baking dish and bake in medium oven—350° F or 175° C—50-60 minutes. Baste with marinade now and then during baking. If desired, a gravy may be made of drippings. Serve with boiled rice and some exotic salad, such as Mixed Salad à la Hawaii or Hawaiian Coleslaw. Serves 4-5.

## SOUTHERN FRIED CHICKEN

| | | |
|---|---|---|
| 1 | (1) | chicken, 2-3 lbs (1-1½ kg, cut into serving pieces) |
| ½ cup | (1 dl) | milk |
| ½ cup | (1 dl) | flour, mixed with ½ cup (1 dl) bread crumbs |
| | | salt and pepper to taste |
| | | For deep frying: shortening or salad oil |

Heat fat in heavy saucepan or large, deep frying pan, using enough to make it about 1″ (2 cm) deep. Dip chicken pieces first in milk, then in flour mixed with breadcrumbs, salt and pepper, then leave them for at least 10 minutes so that they are completely dry. Fry them in hot fat about 10 minutes, and then turn over and cook them on other side another 10 minutes. If desired, more fat can be used so that the pieces of chicken will be completely submerged and do not have to be turned over. However, do not add too many pieces of chicken at a time, as the fat then will cool off too much and cooking time will get much longer and chicken less crisp. When golden brown, remove chicken pieces, let them drain on paper towels for a minute or so, then serve as quickly as possible; otherwise keep them warm in a heated oven, but keep pieces spread out so the crispness does not get lost. Serves 4-5.

## CHICKEN CACCIATORE

*Here is a chicken recipe from sunny Italy that America has taken to its heart. Easy to make and a nice change from other chicken dishes.*

| | | |
|---|---|---|
| 1 | (1) | chicken, 2–3 lbs (1–1½ kg), cut in pieces |
| 2 tbsp | (2 tbsp) | butter or margarine |
| 1 can | (1 can) | tomato soup or 1 can tomatoes (1½ cups— 4 dl) |
| ¼ cup | (½ dl) | water |
| ¼ cup | (½ dl) | dry red wine |
| 1 tbsp | (1 tbsp) | vinegar |
| 1 | (1) | clove garlic, crushed |
| 1 tsp | (1 tsp) | oregano |
| | | salt and pepper to taste |
| ½ | (½) | medium green pepper, chopped |
| ½ cup | (1 dl) | minced onion |

Brown chicken in butter or margarine, brown onion lightly. Add all the remaining ingredients and mix well. Simmer over low heat under cover about 45 minutes, remove cover and if sauce is not sufficiently thick, let simmer for a while without cover until thickened. Serves 4–6.

## CHICKEN DIVAN

On the bottom of a greased, low baking dish place a layer of broccoli, cooked until *almost* tender. On top put a layer of boiled

Chicken Cacciatore and rice

or fried chicken (boned or not), or slices of turkey. Make a white sauce (see page 165) and add ¼ cup (½ dl) Parmesan cheese and 2 tbsp sherry. Remove sauce from heat and add half of it to a slightly beaten egg yolk, then pour all of it back into the sauce pan. Pour this sauce over chicken and broccoli and bake in medium oven—350° F or 175° C for about 20 minutes. The sauce in the above recipe is sufficient for about 4 people and the remaining ingredients should be used in accordance with this. This is a good dish to use when you have leftover chicken or turkey on hand, and it is sufficiently different to take away the "left-over" feeling.

# CHICKEN A LA KING

*Chicken à la King is one of the most popular dishes for large gatherings such as weddings and club luncheons. It can be prepared ahead of time and needs very little work at the time of serving. Professional caterers often substitute turkey for the chicken, without changing the name.*

| | | |
|---|---|---|
| 2 tbsp | (2 tbsp) | butter or margarine |
| ⅔ cup | (1½ dl) | fresh or canned mushrooms, sliced |
| 2 tbsp | (2 tbsp) | green pepper, chopped |
| 4 tbsp | (4 tbsp) | flour |
| 1 tsp | (1 tsp) | salt |
| 1½ cups | (4 dl) | milk |
| 1 cup | (2½ dl) | chicken stock |
| 3 cups | (7–8 dl) | cooked chicken, cubed (see page 94) |
| 1 tbsp | (1 tbsp) | minced parsley |
| 2 | (2) | egg yolks |
| 3 tbsp | (3 tbsp) | sherry |

Sauté mushrooms and green pepper in butter or margarine for about 5 minutes. Add flour and salt and cook, stirring constantly, until smooth, add milk and stock, a little at a time and simmer for about 5 minutes. Add chicken and parsley and let it get warm. Stir in slightly beaten egg yolks and sherry but make sure it does not boil, as the eggs would then curdle. Serve with rice or on top of toast. 5–6 portions.

## CHICKEN PIE

| 1 | (1) | chicken (about 3 lbs–1½ kg) |
|---|-----|------------------------------|

**To cook chicken:**

| 8 cups | (2 l) | water |
|--------|-------|-------|
| 1 tbsp | (1 tbsp) | salt |
| 6-8 | (6-8) | whole pepper corns |
| 1 | (1) | bay leaf |
| 1 | (1) | medium onion, with one clove in it |
| 1 | (1) | carrot |
| | | tops and leaves of a few stalks of celery |

Put all ingredients in a large pot and simmer until chicken is completely tender. Take out chicken, drain and cut into cubes. Make a rather thick sauce out of the following ingredients:

| 3 tbsp | (3 tbsp) | butter or margarine (or skim off fat on top of chicken stock and use this) |
|--------|----------|-----------------------------------------------------------------------------|
| 3 tbsp | (3 tbsp) | flour |
| 1½–2 cups | (6-8 dl) | chicken stock |
| 2 tsp | (2 tsp) | lemon juice |
| 1 tsp | (1 tsp) | sugar |
| 1 cup | (2½ dl) | cooked peas |
| 1 cup | (2½ dl) | cooked carrots |

Melt butter or fat in sauce pan, add flour, stirring constantly, add stock, a little at a time and blend well. Add lemon juice and sugar. The sauce should be rather thick. Add the cut up chicken, peas, and carrots and mix. Pour mixture into a pie pan or low baking dish. Make a "cover" from single pie crust (see page 41). Roll out pie crust to fit the dish, wet edges to fasten crust. Cut out a couple of small center vents so that the steam may escape during baking. Bake in hot oven—425° F or 220° C—about 15 minutes. Serve immediately to 5-6 people.

## CHICKEN BISCUIT CASSEROLE

Proceed in the same manner as for preceding recipe. Instead of pie crust, make biscuits (see page 5) which should be cut into small round buns and placed close together on top of chicken mixture in baking dish. Bake in hot oven—425° F or 220° C—12–15 minutes or until biscuits are baked and golden brown.

## CHICKEN CHOW MEIN

*Like Chop Suey, this is a good dish for left-overs which need to be "stretched" a bit. Either turkey or shrimp can be substituted for the chicken.*

| | | |
|---|---|---|
| ¼ cup | (½ dl) | salad oil |
| ½ cup | (1 dl) | onion, cut in thin slices |
| 1 cup | (2 dl) | celery, cut in thin slices |
| 1 cup | (2 dl) | cabbage, shredded |
| 1 can | (1 can) | mixed chinese vegetables (bean sprouts, water chestnuts, bamboo shoots) or 1 can with only bean sprouts—1½–2 cups (4–5 dl) |
| 1¼ cups | (3 dl) | chicken stock or bouillon (may be made from bouillon cubes) |
| 1½–2 cups | (4–5 dl) | cooked chicken, cut in thin strips |
| 2 tbsp | (2 tbsp) | cornstarch or potato starch |
| ¼ cup | (½ dl) | cold water |
| ¼ cup | (½ dl) | soy sauce |

Sauté onion and celery in oil over low heat for about 10 minutes. Add cabbage, bring to a boil, and simmer for a few minutes more. Add remaining vegetables and stock, then cut chicken and let it all get thoroughly hot. Mix cornstarch with the cold water and stir it into chicken mixture, bring to a boil, then add soy sauce. Eat with boiled rice and Chinese chow mein noodles, if these are obtainable. Serves 4–6.

## CHICKEN RICE ORIENTAL

| | | |
|---|---|---|
| 1 tbsp | (1 tbsp) | finely minced onion |
| 3 tbsp | (3 tbsp) | salad oil |
| 1¼ cups | (3 dl) | cooked chicken, cubed (see page 94) |

| 2 cups | (5 dl) | hot water |
|--------|--------|-----------|
|        |        | salt and pepper to taste |
| 1¼ cups | (3 dl) | Minute rice |
| 1½ cups | (3–4 dl) | lettuce, cut in thin strips |
| 2 tbsp | (2 tbsp) | soy sauce |

Sauté onion in salad oil until wilted. Add chicken, water and rice, salt and pepper to taste and bring to a boil. Cover pan and remove from heat. Let mixture stand for 5 minutes. Just before serving, add lettuce, cut in thin strips, and soy sauce, blending well. Serves 4–5.

## BAKED MACARONI AND CHEESE

*These two ingredients make a natural combination. It used to be a standard Friday meal among Catholics in the United States who did not like fish. But it did not seem to lose any of its popularity when the ban against meat on Fridays was lifted.*

| ½ lb | (¼ kg) | elbow macaroni (about 2 cups) |
|------|--------|-------------------------------|
| 2 tbsp | (2 tbsp) | butter or margarine |
| 1 tbsp | (1 tbsp) | flour |
| ¼ tsp | (¼ tsp) | dry mustard |
| 1 tsp | (1 tsp) | salt |
|       |        | pinch of pepper |
| 2 cups | (5 dl) | milk |
| ½ lb | (¼ kg) | cheese of Cheddar type, cut in thin slices or grated roughly |

Cook macaroni in salted water until tender and drain. Melt butter in a heavy saucepan, mix in flour, stirring constantly, and add milk a little at a time. Add salt and pepper and ¾ of the cheese, keep stirring until cheese is completely melted. Pour in drained macaroni and mix well, then pour mixture into a greased baking dish. Sprinkle with remaining ¼ of cheese and bake in medium hot oven—400° F or 200° C—20 minutes. If this dish is served without anything else with it, it is sufficient for four people, but if it is served instead of potatoes, it is sufficient for 6. If desired, cubed boiled, ham may be added to macaroni mixture before baking.

## CHEESE FONDUE

*This dish resembles a soufflé more than it does the Swiss fondue.*

| | | |
|---|---|---|
| 1 cup | (2½ dl) | milk |
| 1 cup | (2 dl) | bread crumbs |
| ½ lb | (¼ kg) | cheese of Swiss type, roughly grated or cut in fine strips |
| 1 tsp | (1 tsp) | salt |
| 3 | (3) | egg yolks, slightly beaten |
| 3 | (3) | egg whites, beaten until stiff |
| | | pinch of baking powder |

Mix together the first four ingredients. Add egg yolks and mix well. Fold in carefully the stiffly beaten egg whites, mixed with baking powder. Pour into a well greased baking dish and bake in medium oven—350° F or 175° C—30 minutes. Serves 4-5.

## CHEDDAR CHEESE PIE

| | | |
|---|---|---|
| 1 | (1) | unbaked single pie crust (see page 41) |
| 4 | (4) | eggs |
| 1½ cups | (4 dl) | milk |
| ½ lb | (¼ kg) | cheese of Cheddar type |
| | | salt and pepper to taste |
| ⅔ cup | (1½ dl) | boiled ham, cut into cubes |

Grate cheese roughly. Beat eggs lightly and mix with milk, cheese, salt and pepper and ham. Pour mixture in the unbaked pie shell and bake in medium oven—350° F or 175° C—40-45 minutes. Garnish with parsley. Serves 5-6.

## NEW ENGLAND BAKED BEANS

*In the northeast states (New England) baked beans are the classical Saturday night meal. They are so well liked that they are often served just plain, without meat or side dishes. In other parts of the country frankfurters are a standard accompaniment.*

| | | |
|---|---|---|
| 1 lb | (½ kg) | **brown beans, or navy beans or other** |
| ½ lb | (¼ kg) | **salt pork, cut in thick slices** |
| 1 | (1) | **medium onion, sliced** |
| 1 tsp | (1 tsp) | **salt** |
| | | **pepper to taste** |
| ¼ cup | (½ dl) | **molasses** |
| ¼ cup | (½ dl) | **brown sugar** |
| 1 tsp | (1 tsp) | **dry mustard** |
| 4 cups | (1 l) | **boiling water** |

Rinse beans, go over them and take away bad ones, soak them over night. Pour off all water and put them in a heavy sauce pan or kettle. Add all the remaining ingredients and the boiling water. Bring to a boil and turn down heat as much as possible and let them simmer very slowly for 6 hours, or more, until completely tender. Stir now and then carefully, with a wooden spoon, and if they should get too dry, add a little more boiling water. Serves 5-6.

**Variation:**

BAKED BEANS WITH TOMATO FLAVOR

Add ½ cup of ketchup to the above recipe. Otherwise proceed in the same way as described, but in case they should be somewhat sour in flavor, add a little more brown sugar.

## BROCCOLI CASSEROLE WITH DEVILED EGGS AND SHRIMP

| | | |
|---|---|---|
| 6 | (6) | hard boiled eggs |
| 2 tbsp | (2 tbsp) | mayonnaise |
| | | pinch of dry mustard |
| | | pinch of paprika |
| | | salt and pepper to taste |
| ½ lb | (2–3 hg) | boiled shrimp |
| 2 cups | (5 dl) | white sauce (see page 165) |
| ⅔ cup | (1½ dl) | grated cheese of Cheddar type |
| | | fresh or frozen broccoli, amount according to desire |

Shell the hard boiled eggs and cut them in half lengthwise. Remove egg yolks, put into a bowl and mix well with mayonnaise, mustard, paprika, salt and pepper. Fill hollows in whites with this mixture and set aside. Boil broccoli and put in the bottom of a greased baking dish, add a layer of shrimp and set the eggs on top. Pour the white sauce mixed with the grated cheese over shrimp, making sure that the eggs are not covered by the sauce but stick up decoratively in between. Bake in slow oven—325° F or 160° C—30–35 minutes. Serves six.


## ONION SOUP

*Soup is probably most popular as a luncheon dish in America. There are good canned, dried and frozen soups, but recipes for homemade soups, and for improving canned soups, are widely used.*

| | | |
|---|---|---|
| 4–6 | (4–6) | onions, cut in rather thick slices |
| 2 tbsp | (2 tbsp) | butter or margarine |
| 3 cups | (7 dl) | beef stock or water (or bouillon made from cubes) |
| | | salt and pepper to taste |
| 10 | (10) | whole allspice |
| 3 | (3) | slices of toast, cut in quarters |
| | | grated Parmesan cheese |

Brown onion lightly in butter, add stock and spices and simmer until onion is tender. Pour soup into small, deep soup bowls, put 3 pieces of toast on top, cut up into several pieces, and sprinkle generously with grated Parmesan cheese. Put bowls in oven under broiler ½-1 minute to melt cheese. Serve immediately. Four portions.

## CORN CHOWDER

| | | |
|---|---|---|
| 2 oz | (½ hg) | salt pork, diced |
| 1 | (1) | small onion, cut into thin slices |
| 1 | (1) | can whole kernel corn (about 2 cups— 5 dl) |
| 2 cups | (5 dl) | raw potatoes, cut into cubes |
| 1½ cups | (4 dl) | fresh tomatoes, cut into cubes, or 1 can tomatoes |
| 1 tbsp | (1 tbsp) | sugar |
| 1 tsp | (1 tsp) | salt |
| ½ tsp | (½ tsp) | pepper |
| 4 cups | (1 l) | boiling water |
| 1 cup | (2½ dl) | hot milk |

Fry salt pork cubes until golden brown and crisp, add onion and sauté for about 5 minutes. Add vegetables, sugar, salt and pepper and then water and simmer until potatoes are tender. Remove from heat and stir in the hot milk and serve immediately. If desired, crackers may be crumbled into each soup bowl and soup poured on top. Serves 6–8.

## QUICK CORN CHOWDER

| | | |
|---|---|---|
| 1 can | (1 can) | mushroom soup |
| 1 can | (1 can) | whole kernel corn (about 2 cups—5 dl) |
| 4 cups | (1 l) | milk |
| 1 | (1) | small onion, cut into slices |
| 1 tbsp | (1 tbsp) | butter or margarine |
| ½ tsp | (½ tsp) | salt |
| | | pinch of pepper |

Brown onion lightly in butter, stir in mushroom soup, corn and milk. Add salt and pepper and let slowly simmer for about 15 minutes. Serves 6–8.

## AROOSTOOK SOUP

*Aroostook County in Maine is a major center of the potato growing industry, so there is justification for using its name for this hearty, potato-based soup.*

| | | |
|---|---|---|
| 1 cup | (2½ dl) | onion, cut in halves then sliced |
| 1 cup | (2½ dl) | celery, cut into thin slices (or same amount of celeriac, cut into cubes |
| 2 tbsp | (2 tbsp) | butter or margarine |
| 3 cups | (8 dl) | potatoes, cut into cubes |
| 1¼ cups | (3 dl) | water |
| 3 cups | (8 dl) | milk |
| 1 tbsp | (1 tbsp) | flour, stirred with 2 tbsp melted butter |
| 2 tbsp | (2 tbsp) | minced parsley |

Sauté onion and celery in 2 tbsp butter or margarine 10–15 minutes, but do not let it get brown. Add potatoes and water. Simmer until potatoes are tender, then add flour stirred with butter and simmer 5 minutes. Add milk and let it slowly get thoroughly hot, making sure it does not boil, as the milk would curdle. Just before serving, add 2 tbsp minced parsley on top of soup. Five to 6 portions.

# VEGETABLES

Vegetables, in great variety and liberal portions, are a feature of American cooking. Many of them are obtainable fresh all around the year, and most of them are always available in cans or frozen packages. Their finest season is from middle summer to early autumn, when most kinds are plentiful and in prime condition in home gardens, and on vegetable stands and in markets.

Most of the time vegetables are eaten without much preparation, just boiled or steamed. No recipe is required for that, but I have gone on to include a few special treatments which are well worth trying.

Potatoes are considered to be a separate class of vegetable. They may be served boiled, but are more frequently mashed, fried, baked or prepared in other ways. Mashed and fried potatoes seem to be well known all over the world, so no recipes are offered for them. But baked potatoes, which are an American specialty and a top favorite whenever the oven is used for the meal, are both easy to prepare and delicious. I have often wondered why they are not eaten more in other countries.

# BAKED RICE AU GRATIN

| | | |
|---|---|---|
| 1 cup | (2½ dl) | rice |
| 2 cups | (5 dl) | water |
| 2 cups | (5 dl) | white sauce (see page 165) |
| | | pinch of thyme |
| 1 tsp | (1 tsp) | Worcestershire sauce |
| 1 cup | (2½ dl) | grated cheese, preferably Cheddar |
| ¼ cup | (½ dl) | bread crumbs |
| 1 tbsp | (1 tbsp) | butter or margarine |

Cook rice until tender. Add thyme and Worcestershire sauce to white sauce. Put one layer of rice in a greased baking dish, cover with a layer of sauce, then a layer of cheese. Continue with these layers until all ingredients are used up but see to it that on top there is a layer of cheese. On top of this cheese layer, sprinkle bread crumbs and dot with butter. Bake in medium oven—350° F or 175° C—20 minutes or until cheese is thoroughly melted and bread crumbs have a nice golden color. Serves 6.

# SPANISH RICE PRONTO

| | | |
|---|---|---|
| ¼ cup | (½ dl) | bacon grease or butter |
| 1 | (1) | medium onion, thinly sliced |
| ½ | (½) | medium green pepper, cut in small pieces |
| 2 cups | (5 dl) | Minute rice |
| 2 cups | (5 dl) | hot water |
| 1 can | (1 can) | tomato soup |
| 1 tsp | (1 tsp) | salt |
| | | pinch of pepper |
| ½ tsp | (½ tsp) | dry mustard |

Sauté onion in fat until golden in color and tender, add green pepper and Minute rice. Stir over high heat until browned. Add the remaining ingredients and blend well. Bring to a boil, turn down heat and simmer over low heat about 5 minutes. Serves 6.

## SCALLOPED POTATOES

| | | |
|---|---|---|
| 5 | (5) | **medium potatoes, cut in pieces of ¼ x 1″ (½ x 2 cm)** |
| 1 | (1) | **medium onion, sautéed a few minutes in 2 tbsp butter or margarine** |
| | | **salt and pepper to taste** |
| 1 tbsp | (1 tbsp) | **flour** |
| 1 cup, appr | (2–3 dl) | **hot milk** |

Put potato pieces in a greased baking dish, sprinkle with flour, mix in onion and add salt and pepper to taste. Pour over hot milk so that it reaches ½″ (1 cm) from the top of potatoes. Bake uncovered in medium oven—350° F or 175° C—about 1 hour and 15 minutes, or until potatoes are tender. Serves 4–5.

## BAKED POTATOES

*Potatoes can be baked in the oven with a roast, without any extra problem in preparation, making this a good and convenient way to prepare them. Baked potatoes are good to eat with just butter or sour cream, or can be made more fancy by stuffing.*

Use rather large, even, smooth potatoes. Scrub them and dry them well. Bake in hot oven—425° F or 220° C—about 45 minutes or until potatoes feel soft when pressed slightly. Remove from oven, cut an opening in shape of a cross in the middle of each potato and squeeze carefully so that they will open up a bit. Put a pat of butter or some sour cream in the opening, add salt and pepper to taste and serve them piping hot.

## STUFFED POTATOES

Use rather large potatoes. Scrub well and bake them in hot oven—425° F or 220° C—about 45 minutes, or until completely tender. Cut them in halves lengthwise, scoop out their pulp and mix it with one of the following. Each recipe gives amounts for one potato, so multiply quantities by the number of potatoes used.

1. 2 tbsp    boiled ham, cut into very small cubes
   1 tbsp    minced onion
   1 tbsp    minced parsley
            a little milk

2. 2 tbsp    sour cream
   2 tbsp    bacon, broiled or fried and crumbled
   1 tbsp    minced onion

3. 1 tbsp    grated cheese
            a little milk

4. 2 tbsp    sour cream
   1 tbsp    finely chopped cucumber
            salt to taste

5. 2 tbsp    sour cream
   1 tbsp    finely minced dill

Mash potato pulp, add ingredients according to one of the above suggestions and mix well. Add salt and pepper to taste and blend vigorously to make potatoes light and fluffy. Put back into shells, sprinkle with paprika and put back into oven—400° F or 200° C—until golden in color. One or two halves per person.

## POTATOES CHARLOTTE

| 1 | (1) | medium onion, finely minced |
| 3 tbsp | (3 tbsp) | butter or margarine |
| 2 | (2) | slices white bread |

| | | |
|---|---|---|
| 3 cups | (8 dl) | roughly grated potatoes, raw |
| 2 | (2) | eggs, slightly beaten |
| 1 tbsp | (1 tbsp) | salt |
| 1 tsp | (1 tsp) | paprika |

Sauté onion in butter. Soak bread slices in cold water, squeeze out excess water and add to grated potatoes. Then add onion, eggs and spices. Grease a skillet or baking dish, and bake potato mixture in warm oven—400° F or 200° C—until potatoes are tender and have a nice golden color. Serves 5-6.

## FRENCH FRIED ONION RINGS

| | | |
|---|---|---|
| 4–5 | (4–5) | large onions |
| 1 | (1) | egg |
| ⅔ cup | (1½ dl) | flour |
| ½ tsp | (½ tsp) | salt |
| ½ cup | (1 dl) | milk |

Make a batter by beating the egg slightly, adding milk, flour and salt and beating until smooth. Cut onions into rather thick slices, take them apart into rings, dip into batter and put them carefully in very hot fat—375° F or 190° C—and cook them until golden brown—about 2 minutes. Let them drip on paper toweling. Instead of batter, the onion rings may be dipped only in milk and then fried, but they will not be as crisp. Serves 4-5.

# GARDEN JAMBALAYA

*This festive mixture is appropriate for late summer, when there is an abundance of fresh vegetables of all kinds.*

| | | |
|---|---|---|
| 1 | (1) | onion, cut into thin slices |
| 1 cup | (2 dl) | celery, cut into thin slices |
| 3 tbsp | (3 tbsp) | butter or margarine |
| 3 cups | (8 dl) | fresh vegetables (string beans, cucumbers, green peppers and tomatoes) |
| 2 cups | (5 dl) | hot bouillon (may be made from cubes) |
| 1 tsp | (1 tsp) | salt |
| | | pinch of pepper |
| 1 tbsp | (1 tbsp) | fresh lemon juice |
| 1 tbsp | (1 tbsp) | corn starch (or potato starch) mixed with 2 tbsp. water |
| 1 cup | (3 dl) | Minute rice |

Sauté onion and celery in butter in a large frying pan until tender, but make sure it does not get brown. Add the remaining vegetables and half of the hot bouillon. Add salt and pepper to taste, and lemon juice. Pour in starch mixed with water and stir until well blended. Make a well in the middle of vegetables and pour Minute rice in this, pour in remaining bouillon and make sure rice is completely covered by the liquid. Cover and let mixture simmer 5–10 minutes. Serve directly from frying pan. Serves 6–8.

# BAKED CUCUMBERS IN SOUR CREAM

Place thick cucumber slices in a greased baking dish. Add salt and pepper to taste, then minced parsley or chives. Bake in medium oven—350° F or 175° C—for about 10 minutes. Take out of oven and add sufficient sour cream to make a sauce, then bake for a few minutes more, or until cucumbers are completely tender. (The quantities in this recipe are completely dependent upon how many portions you wish to make etc.).

# BAKED STRING BEAN CASSEROLE

| | | |
|---|---|---|
| 1 can | (1 can) | string beans (about 1½ cup—4 dl) or cooked fresh ones in the same amount |
| 1 can | (1 can) | mushroom soup |
| ¼ cup | (½ dl) | bread crumbs |
| 1 tbsp | (1 tbsp) | butter or margarine |
| | *or* | |
| 1 | (1) | large onion, french-fried in rings, instead of bread crumbs and butter |

Drain beans and pour them in a greased baking dish and pour mushroom soup over them. Sprinkle with bread crumbs, dot with butter. Instead of bread crumbs, you may use a layer of french-fried onion rings (see recipe page 105). Bake in medium oven—350° F or 175° C—15-20 minutes and serve immediately. Serves 5-6.

# CORN FRITTERS

*These fritters can replace both potato and vegetable as an accompaniment to meat. They are particularly good for enlivening a meal in which the main dish is not particularly interesting.*

| | | |
|---|---|---|
| 1 cup | (2½ dl) | flour |
| 1 tsp | (1 tsp) | salt |
| 1 tsp | (1 tsp) | baking powder |
| 2 | (2) | eggs, slightly beaten |
| ¼ cup | (½ dl) | milk |
| 1 can | (1 can) | whole kernel corn, well drained (about 2 cups—5 dl) |
| 1 tbsp | (1 tbsp) | melted butter or margarine |

Sift together flour, salt and baking powder. Mix eggs with milk and add to the dry ingredients and stir until batter is smooth. Add corn and the melted butter or margarine. Heat ½″ (1 cm) of salad oil or shortening in frying pan to 400° F or 200° C and drop batter by tablespoonfuls in hot fat, but not too many at a time as they then will not turn out as crisp. Turn over when golden brown on one side and fry other side. If desired, more fat may be used so that fritters are completely covered. When ready, drain off excess grease on paper toweling and serve fritters piping hot with butter, jam or maple syrup. They are good with fried pork or ham. Serves 5–6.

## CORN CAKES

| | | |
|---|---|---|
| 1 cup | (2½ dl) | canned whole kernel corn, well drained |
| 1 | (1) | egg, slightly beaten |
| ¼ cup | (½ dl) | flour |
| 1 tsp | (1 tsp) | salt |
| | | pinch of pepper |

Mix flour with corn, stir in egg and add salt and pepper to taste. Make cakes of about 1 tbsp. batter and fry in butter or oil on both sides until golden brown. Serves 4–5.

## CORN PUDDING

| | | |
|---|---|---|
| 1 can | (1 can) | whole kernel corn, about 2 cups (5 dl) |
| 3 | (3) | eggs, slightly beaten |
| ¼ cup | (½ dl) | flour |
| 1 tsp | (1 tsp) | salt |
| | | pepper to taste |
| 1 tbsp | (1 tbsp) | sugar |
| | | pinch of nutmeg |
| 2 tbsp | (2 tbsp) | butter or margarine, melted |
| 1⅔ cups | (4 dl) | milk and cream, mixed |

Put corn and eggs in a large bowl and mix well. Stir together flour, salt, pepper, sugar and nutmeg and add to corn mixture. Then add melted butter and milk and blend well. Pour in a greased baking dish and put same in the oven in a larger dish, filled up to about 1″ with water. Bake in slow oven—325° F or 165° C—until pudding is done. Test with a sharp knife stuck into the middle of pudding, and when knife comes out dry, the pudding is done. Serves 8.

## ZESTY CARROTS

*Plain carrots are good, we know, but try this unusual way to prepare them for a delicious change.*

| | | |
|---|---|---|
| 6–8 | (6–8) | cooked carrots, cut into long thin strips |
| ¼ cup | (½ dl) | water or liquid from carrots |
| 2 tbsp | (2 tbsp) | grated onion |
| 2 tbsp | (2 tbsp) | grated horse-radish |
| ½ cup | (1 dl) | mayonnaise |
| | | salt and pepper to taste |
| ¼ cup | (½ dl) | bread crumbs |
| 1 tbsp | (1 tbsp) | butter |
| | | pinch of paprika |

Put carrot strips in a low baking dish. Mix together liquid from boiling carrots, grated onion, horse-radish, mayonnaise and salt and pepper to taste. Pour over carrots. Sprinkle bread crumbs on top, dot with butter and sprinkle with paprika. Bake in medium hot oven—375° F or 190° C—15–20 minutes. Garnish with minced parsley. Serves 6.

# RICE STUFFED TOMATOES

| | | |
|---|---|---|
| 6 | (6) | medium tomatoes |
| ½ cup | (1¼ dl) | rice |
| 1 tsp | (1 tsp) | salt |
| | | pepper and paprika to taste |
| 1 can | (1 can) | peas, well drained (about 1 cup—3 dl) |
| 1 cup | (3 dl) | grated sharp cheese, Cheddar type |

Put tomatoes in boiling water for one minute, pour off water, and skin. Cut a thin slice off stem end of tomato and with a spoon, scoop out pulp.

**Filling:** Boil rice in 1¼ cup (3 dl) water. When tender, pour off any excess water, then mix rice with salt, pepper, paprika and peas. Add ¾ cup (1¾ dl) cheese and mix carefully so as not to crush peas. Add filling to tomatoes and sprinkle with remaining cheese. Place tomatoes in a greased baking dish and pour ½ cup (1¼ dl) of water in the bottom of dish. Bake in medium oven—350° F or 175° C—25–30 minutes or until tomatoes are completely tender. Remove with a slotted utensil and put on serving dish. Garnish with parsley sprigs. Serves 6.

# HARVARD BEETS

| | | |
|---|---|---|
| 1 tbsp | (1 tbsp) | cornstarch or potato starch |
| 2 tbsp | (2 tbsp) | water |
| 3 tbsp | (3 tbsp) | butter or margarine, melted |
| ¼ cup | (½ dl) | vinegar (or more if a stronger taste is desired) |
| 2 tbsp | (2 tbsp) | sugar |
| 1 tsp | (1 tsp) | grated onion |
| | | salt and pepper to taste |
| 2 lbs | (1 kg) | small beets, boiled and peeled |

Mix together cornstarch and water and stir in melted butter. Add vinegar and heat carefully, stirring constantly until mixture comes to a boil and thickens. Add sugar, spices and beets and let beets get thoroughly hot. Serves 6.

## SPINACH AND EGG CASSEROLE

| | | |
|---|---|---|
| 1 lb | (½ kg) | fresh spinach (or one package frozen spinach, about 10 oz.—3 hg) |
| 1 tbsp | (1 tbsp) | fresh lemon juice |
| 3 | (3) | hard boiled eggs, cut in slices |
| 2 tbsp | (2 tbsp) | butter or margarine |
| ¼ cup | (½ dl) | grated cheese, Swiss type |
| ½ cup | (1 dl) | grated Parmesan cheese |

Rinse and clean spinach and cook in sauce pan over very low heat about 5 minutes, until wilted. (Do not add extra water, it is sufficient with water that clings to leaves after rinsing). Pour off excess liquid and put spinach in a greased baking dish, sprinkle with lemon juice, and put egg slices on top.

Make a white sauce (see page 166), add pinch of nutmeg, grated Swiss cheese, and half of Parmesan cheese. Pour sauce over spinach and eggs and sprinkle with remaining Parmesan cheese. Bake without cover in warm oven—375° F or 190° C—about 20 minutes, or until casserole is golden in color. 4–5 servings.

# SOY SAUCE RICE

| | | |
|---|---|---|
| 1 cup | (2½ dl) | rice |
| 2 cups | (5 dl) | water |
| 2 tbsp | (2 tbsp) | salad oil |
| 3 tbsp | (3 tbsp) | soy sauce |
| 2 tbsp | (2 tbsp) | finely minced onion |
| 1 tsp | (1 tsp) | sugar |

Boil rice in water under cover about 20 minutes, or until tender. Remove from heat and let stand for 20 minutes. Stir with a fork so that it does not stick together and mix in remaining ingredients. Heat carefully and serve. For 4 people.

# FRIED TOMATOES

*If you grow your own tomatoes, you can use this recipe both for ripe ones in the summer, and for green ones left on hand after the first frost.*

| | | |
|---|---|---|
| 6 | (6) | medium tomatoes, ripe or green |
| 1 | (1) | egg |
| ½ cup | (1 dl) | bread crumbs |
| ½ tsp | (½ tsp) | salt |
| | | pepper to taste |

Cut tomatoes in ½″ (1 cm) thick slices. Beat egg lightly and add salt and pepper to taste. Dip tomato slices in bread crumbs, then into the egg and then into bread crumbs again. Fry in butter or margarine, until nicely brown on both sides. Serves 6.

# SALADS

Salads are a very important part of many meals in the United States. Fresh ingredients are available the year round, and in addition, there are many salads that do not require perishable fresh materials. These include jellied or molded salads, and varieties using canned or frozen vegetables and fruit.

American salads are of equal importance as side dishes and as courses in dinners, and as main dishes for lunch. Most of them are very interesting to people who are interested in keeping calories to a minimum. They may permit a really satisfactory amount of eating, without providing much building material for waistlines. Others, equally pleasant to eat, are full meals in every sense of the word.

Salads are most appreciated in hot weather, but are served throughout the year. They offer a variety of texture, flavor and color which cannot be brought to meals in any other way.

I have included a few basic recipes for salad dressings. You can make a big batch of any one of these, and then vary it with different flavorings so that you can appear to have a wide variety of dressing on hand.

## SPINACH SALAD

*Fresh spinach is often used in salads in the United States, but it does not seem to be used uncooked elsewhere, in spite of its wide availability in many countries.*

**Spinach Salad, continued**

| | | |
|---|---|---|
| ½ lb | (¼ kg) | spinach, rinsed and dried, torn into small pieces |
| 1 | (1) | small onion, thinly sliced |
| ¼ cup | (½ dl) | chopped celery |
| 4 | (4) | hard boiled eggs, sliced |
| | | salt and pepper to taste |

Mix together the above ingredients carefully and chill well. Prepare the following dressing:

| | | |
|---|---|---|
| 1 tbsp | (1 tbsp) | salad oil |
| 2 tbsp | (2 tbsp) | flour |
| ½ cup | (1¼ dl) | water |
| 1 | (1) | egg yolk |
| ½ tsp | (½ tsp) | dry mustard |
| 2 tbsp | (2 tbsp) | fresh lemon juice |
| ½ tsp | (½ tsp) | salt |
| ¼ tsp | (¼ tsp) | paprika |
| ½ cup | (1 dl) | salad oil |

Mix together first three ingredients in a saucepan and bring to a boil, stirring constantly. Remove from heat and mix in remaining ingredients. Cool, and stir briskly before using.

## ONION ORANGE SALAD BOWL

| | | |
|---|---|---|
| 2 | (2) | medium red onions, thinly sliced |
| 3 | (3) | oranges, thinly sliced |
| ½ lb | (2 hg) | fresh spinach |
| 2 tbsp | (2 tbsp) | french dressing (see page 134) |

Pour dressing over onion and oranges and mix well. Let stand in refrigerator at least one hour. In the meantime rinse and dry spinach and cut away tough parts. Tear into small pieces and put into a plastic bag and keep refrigerated until ready to use. Just before serving, mix spinach with oranges and onions in a large salad bowl. Serves 6–8.

## CAESAR SALAD

*This salad is a little complicated to make, but it is good enough to be worth some trouble. With the addition of sardines it can be used as a main luncheon dish in the summer.*

| | | |
|---|---|---|
| 1 cup | (3 dl) | white bread, cut into ½″ (1 cm) cubes |
| ¼ cup | (½ dl) | salad oil |
| 1 | (1) | clove garlic, or 1 tsp. garlic salt |
| 1 | (1) | head of lettuce |
| 6 | (6) | anchovy fillets, finely chopped |
| ½ cup | (1 dl) | grated Parmesan cheese |
| ¼ cup | (½ dl) | crumbled Roquefort cheese |
| 1 | (1) | raw egg |
| ¼ cup | (½ dl) | fresh lemon juice |
| ¼ cup | (½ dl) | french dressing (see page 134) |

Take apart a head of lettuce, rinse in cold water, dry and tear into pieces. Place leaves in plastic bag in refrigerator for at least half an hour. In the meantime, brown bread cubes lightly in salad oil, to which crushed garlic or garlic salt has been added. Put the chopped anchovies in french dressing and mix well. Just before serving, put lettuce in a bowl, pour dressing over it and sprinkle with the grated and the crumbled cheese. Pour the raw egg in the middle of salad, pour lemon juice on top and mix well. Add the browned and cooled bread cubes, toss and serve immediately. For 6–8 portions.

**Variation:**

To the above salad a can of small whole sardines in oil may be added.

# WALDORF SALAD

*This is a crisp, zesty salad that is especially good with pork or ham.*

| | | |
|---|---|---|
| 2 cups | (5 dl) | apple pieces (about 3 apples, not peeled) |
| 1 cup | (2½ dl) | chopped celery |
| | | chopped nuts, as much as desired |
| 3–4 tbsp | (3–4 tbsp) | mayonnaise |
| | | lettuce |

Mix all ingredients well and add a little whipped cream to mayonnaise if desired. Put on crisp lettuce leaves. Makes 6 servings.

# HAWAIIAN SALAD BOWL

| | | |
|---|---|---|
| 10 | (10) | marshmallows |
| 1 cup | (3 dl) | sour cream |
| 6 | (6) | slices fresh or canned pineapple, cut up |
| 1 | (1) | small can mandarin oranges, well drained |
| ½ cup | (1 dl) | shredded coconut |
| | | lettuce |

Cut each marshmallow into four pieces, mix with sour cream, pineapple, mandarin oranges and coconut and let stand in cool place for several hours. Place on crisp lettuce leaves. Makes 6 servings.

# CHEF'S SALAD

*This salad is often served as a luncheon dish, both in restaurants and at home. It fills a need, for it is not rich in calories but still satisfies the appetite.*

| 1 | (1) | head of lettuce, cut into thin strips |
| ½ cup | (1 dl) | cold chicken, cut into thin strips |
| ½ cup | (1 dl) | boiled ham, cut into thin strips |
| ½ cup | (1 dl) | cheese, Swiss type, cut into thin strips |
| 2 | (2) | hard boiled eggs, quartered |
| 1 | (1) | large (or 2 small) tomatoes, cut into wedges |

Dressing:

| 1 tbsp | (1 tbsp) | minced chives |
| 2 tbsp | (2 tbsp) | finely chopped dill or sweet pickles |
| 3 tbsp | (3 tbsp) | mayonnaise |
| 2 tbsp | (2 tbsp) | vinegar |
| 3 tbsp | (3 tbsp) | salad oil |
| 1 tbsp | (1 tbsp) | Worcestershire sauce |

Put lettuce in the bottom of a large salad bowl. On top of this put piles of chicken, boiled ham, cheese, each by itself, garnish with egg and tomato wedges, and chill. When ready to serve, bring the bowl to the table in this way and keep salad dressing in a separate dish. Just before serving, pour dressing carefully over salad and toss lightly to get everything mixed. Serves 5–6.

Chef's Salad

## GREEN BEAN SALAD

*An easy-to-do salad when you do not have the usual fresh salad ingre-
dients. It is excellent with cold meats, particularly ham.*

| | | |
|---|---|---|
| 1 can | (1 can) | string beans (about 2 cups) or similar amount of fresh ones |
| ½ | (½) | medium onion, thinly sliced |
| 2–3 tbsp | (2–3 tbsp) | french dressing (see page 134) |

If canned beans are used, heat them, and if fresh ones are used
boil them until tender. Drain, and put in salad bowl. Pour dressing
over them and let stand for a few hours in refrigerator. Just before
serving, add sliced onion and mix carefully. For 5–6.

## THREE-BEAN SALAD

| | | |
|---|---|---|
| 1 cup | (2½ dl) | french dressing (see page 134) |
| 1 tbsp | (1 tbsp) | Worcestershire sauce |
| 1 can | (1 can) | cut waxbeans, drained (about 2 cups— 5 dl) |
| 1 can | (1 can) | cut green beans, drained (about 2 cups— 5 dl) |
| 1½ cups | (4 dl) | kidney beans, boiled and drained |
| ⅔ cup | (1½ dl) | finely chopped dill or sweet pickles |
| ½ cup | (1 dl) | red onion, thinly sliced |

In a large bowl mix together dressing, Worcestershire sauce and
beans and mix carefully. Let mixture stand in refrigerator at least
four hours. Just before serving, add chopped pickles and sliced
onion. Serve on lettuce leaves. 8–10 portions.

## BEAN SALAD

| | | |
|---|---|---|
| 2 cups | (5 dl) | cooked and well drained kidney beans |
| ¼ cup | (½ dl) | chopped celery |

Top: Boiled Dinner, page 61
Bottom: Spaghetti and meat balls, pages 77 and 78

| ½ cup | (1 dl) | chopped dill or sweet pickles |
|---|---|---|
| 1 | (1) | small chopped onion |
| 2 | (2) | hard boiled eggs, cut into small pieces |
| | | salt and pepper to taste |
| ¼ cup | (½ dl) | mayonnaise or sour cream |

Mix all ingredients carefully. Do not stir too much as this might break up beans. Chill for several hours. Serve bean salad on lettuce leaves and garnish with a little grated cheese. For 6.

## PEA SALAD

| 1 can | (1 can) | small green peas (Petit points)—about 2 cups (5 dl) |
|---|---|---|
| 1 tbsp | (1 tbsp) | fresh lemon juice |
| 1 | (1) | finely chopped hard boiled egg |
| 2-3 tbsp | (2-3 tbsp) | mayonnaise (mixed with 1 tbsp whipped cream, if desired) |
| | | chopped parsley |

Mix together mayonnaise, (cream), egg and lemon juice in a bowl and add the well drained peas. Carefully mix together and let stand in refrigerator at least 3 hours. Stir carefully again just before serving and sprinkle with chopped parsley. Serves 4.

## COLE SLAW

*Cole slaw is very popular, particularly for serving with fried or boiled fish. Its principal ingredient is fresh cabbage, which is easy to have on hand the year round.*

| ½ | (½) | medium head of cabbage, shredded—about 4 cups (1 l) shredded cabbage |
|---|---|---|
| 2 tbsp | (2 tbsp) | vinegar |
| 1 tbsp | (1 tbsp) | sugar |
| | | salt and pepper to taste |
| 3 tbsp | (3 tbsp) | mayonnaise |

Top: Chicken Cacciatore with rice, page 90
Bottom: Chef's Salad, page 116

Put shredded cabbage in a large bowl with ice water and let stand for about 30 minutes. Drain water and dry cabbage with clean towel. Add sugar, vinegar, salt and pepper and let stand for about 1 hour, then drain excess liquid. Just before serving, add mayonnaise and mix well. Serves 4–5.

## CREAMY COLESLAW

| 1 | (1) | medium cabbage—about 8 cups shredded cabbage (about 2 l) |
|---|---|---|
| ¼ cup | (½ dl) | vinegar |
| 2 tbsp | (2 tbsp) | sugar |
| ½ tsp | (½ tsp) | salt |
| | | pinch of pepper and paprika |
| ½ cup | (1 dl) | chopped green pepper |
| 2 tbsp | (2 tbsp) | chopped sweet red pepper |
| ¼ cup | (½ dl) | mayonnaise |
| ¼ cup | (½ dl) | whipped cream |

Shred cabbage and let stand in ice water for about 30 minutes. Drain and dry cabbage with clean towel. Add vinegar, sugar, salt, pepper and paprika. Mix lightly and let cabbage stand in this marinade 1 hour. Pour off liquid and add chopped green and red peppers. Whip cream, mix it with mayonnaise and add to cabbage mixture, blending well. Serve immediately. For 6–8 portions.

## HAWAIIAN COLESLAW

| ½ | (½) | medium head of cabbage—about 4 cups (1 l) shredded cabbage |
|---|---|---|
| ½ cup | (1 dl) | crushed pineapple |
| 3 tbsp | (3 tbsp) | mayonnaise |

Shred cabbage and let stand in ice water about 30 minutes. Drain, mix cabbage with crushed pineapple and mayonnaise and serve immediately. Serves 5–6.

## SOUR CREAM CUCUMBERS

| | | |
|---|---|---|
| 2 cups | (5 dl) | fresh cucumbers, thinly sliced |
| 1½ tbsp | (1½ tbsp) | vinegar |
| 1 tsp | (1 tsp) | salt |
| | | dash of pepper |
| 1 tbsp | (1 tbsp) | sugar |
| 1 cup | (2½ dl) | sour cream |
| 1 tbsp | (1 tbsp) | chopped chives |
| 2 tbsp | (2 tbsp) | chopped dill |
| ½ tsp | (½ tsp) | dry mustard |

Mix together vinegar, salt, sugar and sour cream, then add pepper, chives, dill and mustard, and mix well. Pour sauce over sliced cucumber, mix lightly and let stand in refrigerator 2-3 hours before serving. Makes 5-6 portions.

## GELATIN SALAD

| | | |
|---|---|---|
| 1 pkg | (1 pkg) | Jello (or similar) gelatin powder, lemon or orange flavor |
| 2 | (2) | carrots, grated |
| 1 | (1) | small piece of cabbage, grated (or fine-cut) |
| 1 cup | (2½ dl) | crushed pineapple |

Mix gelatin with 1 cup (2½ dl) boiling water, and blend well. Add ½ cup (1 dl) cold water and mix. Add vegetables and pineapple (the vegetables may be ground in a meat grinder instead of grated—this is a quicker procedure), and mix until well blended. Pour into a ring mold and refrigerate at least 2 hours. Unmold on serving platter, garnish with lettuce leaves or parsley and place a small bowl with mayonnaise in the middle of the ring to be served with the salad. Makes about 8 servings.

This salad may be made in many variations and with different vegetables in accordance with what you have on hand—for example chopped cucumbers, chopped celery, chopped peppers etc. Also fresh fruits may be added to great advantage, such as oranges cut into small pieces, finely chopped apples etc.

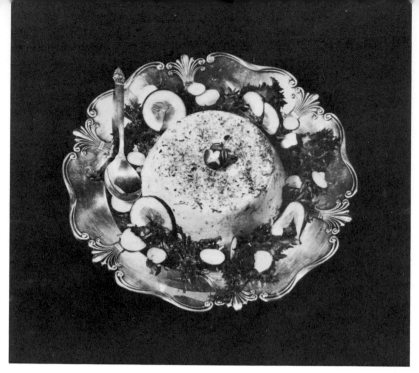

Cucumber Mold

## CUCUMBER MOLD

*A beautiful and delicious gelatin salad which is especially enjoyable on a hot summer day, as its pale green color is as cool and refreshing as its taste.*

| | | |
|---|---|---|
| 2 cups | (5 dl) | fresh cucumbers, cut into small cubes |
| 1 pkg | (1 pkg) | Jello with lime or lemon flavor |
| 1 cup | (2½ dl) | boiling water |
| 1 cup | (2½ dl) | sour cream |
| 2 tbsp | (2 tbsp) | sugar |
| | | paprika |

Dissolve gelatin in boiling water, mix well, let cool until somewhat thickened, stir vigorously and add the remaining ingredients except paprika. If lemon Jello is used, add a few drops of green food coloring in order to get a nice cool color when mixing with the sour cream. Pour mixture in an oiled mold and refrigerate until completely firm. Unmold carefully and sprinkle with a little paprika for color contrast. Serves 8.

# CRANBERRY MOLD

*A flavorful and refreshing gelatin salad, which goes particularly well with turkey or chicken. Cranberries, which are the American equivalent of lingenberries, are almost always served in some form with turkey.*

| | | |
|---|---|---|
| 1 | (1) | orange |
| 2 cups | (5 dl) | lingenberry jam (or whole cranberries) |
| 1 | (1) | small can crushed pineapple |
| 1 cup | (3 dl) | water |
| 1 pkg | (1 pkg) | Jello (strawberry, raspberry or cherry flavor) |
| ¼ cup | (½ dl) | chopped nuts or almonds |

Rinse orange, quarter and take out pits, then grind it, peel and all, in a meat grinder. Mix orange pulp with lingenberries (cranberries) and pineapple. Pour ¾ cup (2 dl) boiling water over Jello and mix well, add ¼ cup (1 dl) cold water and refrigerate until slightly thickened. Stir vigorously and add fruit mixture and nuts. Pour in an oiled mold and chill until completely firm. Unmold carefully on a platter and garnish with lettuce leaves and orange slices. Serves about 8.


# JELLIED PINEAPPLE SALAD

| | | |
|---|---|---|
| 1 can | (1 can) | pineapple, about 10 slices |
| 1 tbsp | (1 tbsp) | gelatin powder |
| ¼ cup | (½ dl) | cold water |
| 2 | (2) | drops food color (optional) |

Dissolve gelatin powder in cold water. Pour juice from pineapple can in a saucepan and bring to a boil, but let slices remain in can. Add dissolved gelatin to hot juice and mix well, then pour it back into the can and refrigerate 2–3 hours. When mixture is completely firm, open pineapple can completely on both sides and carefully push out slices of pineapple with gelatin. Slice and put on serving platter. Food coloring may be added to pineapple juice in order to get a color contrast between gelatin and slices. Serves 6–8.

# BROCCOLI SALAD

*Although made from a humble vegetable, this salad looks festive and is excellent with cold meat or fish.*

| | | |
|---|---|---|
| 1 cup | (3 dl) | clear bouillon or consommé |
| 2 tbsp | (2 tbsp) | gelatin powder |
| 2 pkgs | (2 pkgs) | frozen broccoli, cut into small pieces |
| 6 | (6) | hard boiled eggs, chopped |
| 1 cup | (2½ dl) | mayonnaise |
| 1 tsp | (1 tsp) | Worcestershire sauce |
| 2 tsp | (2 tsp) | fresh lemon juice |

Dissolve gelatin powder in ¼ cup (½ dl) cold water. Bring bouillon to a boil and then add gelatin. Cook broccoli only until the pieces fall apart, then drain and add to bouillon mixture. Mix in remaining ingredients and pour in a large mold (about 8 cups—2 l). Chill until mixture is completely firm, about 2 hours. Unmold carefully and garnish with parsley and tomato wedges. Serves about 8.

# TOMATO ASPIC

*This is a nice salad dish for the summer. If you make it in a ring mold you can fill the center with shrimp, crab, tuna or similar salad. If you add a circle of deviled eggs (page 51) around the outside, you have a whole good meal on one platter.*

| | | |
|---|---|---|
| 2 cups | (5 dl) | canned tomato juice |
| ¼ cup | (½ dl) | cold water |
| 2 tbsp | (2 tbsp) | gelatin powder |
| ¼ cup | (½ dl) | fresh lemon juice |
| 2 tsp | (2 tsp) | sugar |
| 1 | (1) | bay leaf |
| 1 | (1) | thick onion slice |
| ½ tsp | (½ tsp) | Worcestershire sauce |
| 6 | (6) | pepper corns |

Dissolve gelatin in cold water. Mix the remaining ingredients and bring to almost a boil and simmer for about 5 minutes. Remove from heat and add gelatin, stir until well mixed and completely dissolved. Strain mixture and pour into ring mold, or individual molds, chill until completely firm. Unmold carefully on crisp lettuce leaves. Serves 6.

## BEET SALAD CARDINAL

*A salad with real MAN'S taste. It is strong in flavor and color and makes a welcome addition to the Christmas table.*

| | | |
|---|---|---|
| 1 pkg | (1 pkg) | Jello (or similar) gelatin powder with lemon flavor |
| 1 cup | (2½ dl) | boiling water |
| ⅔ cup | (1½ dl) | beet juice |
| 3 tbsp | (3 tbsp) | vinegar |
| 2 tbsp | (2 tbsp) | grated onion |
| 2 cups | (5 dl) | roughly grated beets (or cut into fine strips—julienne), well drained |
| ½ tsp | (½ tsp) | salt |
| 2 tbsp | (2 tbsp) | grated horse-radish |

Dissolve gelatin in boiling water, add beet juice and vinegar. Chill mixture until somewhat thickened. Add remaining ingredients and pour into mold and chill until mixture is completely firm. Carefully unmold on serving platter and garnish with crisp lettuce leaves or parsley, serve with mayonnaise on the side, to about 10.

## SALMON MOUSSE

| | | |
|---|---|---|
| 1 can | (1 can) | 1 lb (5–6 hg) red salmon, or two small cans |
| ¼ cup | (½ dl) | vinegar |
| ¼ cup | (½ dl) | sour cream |
| 1 tbsp | (1 tbsp) | grated horse-radish |
| 1 tbsp | (1 tbsp) | gelatin powder |
| ¼ cup | (½ dl) | fresh lemon juice |
| 1 tsp | (1 tsp) | salt |
| 1 tsp | (1 tsp) | dry mustard |
| ½ cup | (1¼ dl) | heavy cream |

Broccoli Salad

Drain salmon and remove bones and skin. Put salmon in a large bowl and break up into small pieces. Mix with vinegar, ⅓ of it at a time and stir mixture vigorously so that you get a smooth purée. Mix in sour cream and horse-radish. Pour gelatin over lemon juice, mixed with ¼ cup (½ dl) cold water, and let it stand 5 minutes to dissolve, then put it over boiling water to soften. Add completely dissolved gelatin little by little into salmon purée, add salt and mustard and mix well. Carefully fold in the whipped cream. Pour mixture either in individual molds or a large mold, which have been brushed with oil, and put in refrigerator, preferably overnight. Carefully unmold on crisp lettuce leaves, garnish with parsley, tomatoes or lemon wedges. Serves 6.

## MOLDED SALMON SALAD

| | | |
|---|---|---|
| 1 tbsp | (1 tbsp) | gelatin powder |
| ¼ cup | (½ dl) | cold water |
| 1 pkg | (1 pkg) | Jello with lemon flavor |
| 2 cups | (5 dl) | boiling water |
| 1 cup | (2½ dl) | cold water |
| ⅓ cup | (¾ dl) | fresh lemon juice |
| 1 can | (1 can) | red salmon (about 2 cups—5 dl) or two small cans with the same amount |
| ½ tsp | (½ tsp) | salt |
| | | pinch of pepper |

| | | |
|---|---|---|
| 1 tsp | (1 tsp) | grated horse-radish |
| ⅔ cup | (1½ dl) | chopped celery |
| ½ cup | (1 dl) | chopped cucumber |

Soften gelatin powder in ¼ cup (½ dl) cold water, then add Jello and boiling water, stirring until completely dissolved. Add cold water, lemon juice, salmon and spices. Cool mixture until syrupy, then add chopped celery and cucumber and pour into a mold, brushed with salad oil. Cool until gelatin is completely firm. Unmold carefully, garnish with fresh dill or parsley and serve with mayonnaise, to which a little grated onion has been added. Serves 6.

## CHICKEN SALAD IN MOLDED EGG RING

| | | |
|---|---|---|
| 2 tbsp | (2 tbsp) | gelatin powder |
| ½ cup | (1¼ dl) | cold water |
| ½ cup | (1¼ dl) | boiling water |
| 1 cup | (3 dl) | mayonnaise |
| 4 tbsp | (4 tbsp) | fresh lemon juice |
| ½ tsp | (½ tsp) | salt |
| | | a few drops of tabasco |
| 1 tsp | (1 tsp) | grated onion |
| ½ | (½) | medium green pepper, chopped |
| 2 tbsp | (2 tbsp) | minced parsley |
| 12 | (12) | hard boiled eggs |
| | | Chicken salad, see page 131 |

Soften gelatin powder in cold water and let stand 5 minutes. Pour in boiling water and mix, let cool. Add mayonnaise, lemon juice, salt, tabasco, onion, green pepper, parsley and 10 eggs, chopped. Pour a little of this mixture in the bottom of a ring mold and cut the remaining two eggs in slices and put around the edge. Put in refrigerator and let stand until mixture is slightly firm. Carefully add remaining mixture and refrigerate until completely firm. Unmold gently on a serving platter and fill the middle with chicken salad and garnish with tomato wedges. Serve with mayonnaise or French dressing. 8–10 portions.

# EGG SALAD

*A tasty, nourishing salad. It is good in sandwiches, too. But do not make them far in advance, as the bread becomes soggy easily.*

| | | |
|---|---|---|
| 3 | (3) | eggs |
| ⅔ cup | (1½ dl) | chopped celery, or cucumber |
| ½ tsp | (½ tsp) | paprika |
| ½ tsp | (½ tsp) | dry mustard |
| | | salt and pepper to taste |
| 3 tbsp | (3 tbsp) | mayonnaise |

Hard boil eggs, chop them and add remaining ingredients. Put on lettuce leaves or in sandwiches. Serves 4.

# POTATO SALAD

*During the Summer, potato salad is so popular that it is hard to imagine an American picnic without it. It is served most with cold meat, grilled franks and hamburgers; but is good with practically everything.*

| | | |
|---|---|---|
| 2 lbs | (1 kg) | potatoes, preferably small and even in size |
| ¼ cup | (½ dl) | minced onion |
| 3 tbsp | (3 tbsp) | vinegar |
| 3 tbsp | (3 tbsp) | salad oil |
| 2 | (2) | hard boiled eggs |
| | | salt and pepper to taste |
| 3 tbsp | (3 tbsp) | mayonnaise |

Boil potatoes in their jackets but make sure they do not cook too long and get mushy. Peel them and cut into small pieces. When about half the potatoes have been cut and put into a large bowl, add 1½ tbsp vinegar and 1½ tbsp salad oil and half the minced onion, and one finely chopped egg. Proceed peeling the remainder of the potatoes and add remaining vinegar, salad oil, onion and egg, mixing carefully with a wooden spoon so as not to crush potatoes. Add mayonnaise and blend gently. It is important that the potatoes should be warm when preparing this salad, as they will otherwise not absorb the different flavors as well. Other ingredients such as chopped dill, chives, green pepper or celery may be added, in quantities as desired. Cool thoroughly before serving. For 6–8 people.

## POTATO SALAD WITH SOUR CREAM

| | | |
|---|---|---|
| 5 | (5) | medium potatoes |
| ¼ cup | (½ dl) | sour cream |
| ½ cup | (1 dl) | mayonnaise |
| 2 tbsp | (2 tbsp) | chopped green pepper |
| 1 tbsp | (1 tbsp) | minced onion |

Boil potatoes in their jackets but do not let them get soft. In the meantime, in a big bowl mix together sour cream and mayonnaise, adding a little salt, if desired. Mix in green pepper and onion. Peel potatoes, while still hot, and cut into pieces and mix with sour cream mixture. Cool at least 1 hour and mix once more just before eating. Serves 4–5.

## POTATO SALAD CALIFORNIA METHOD

| | | |
|---|---|---|
| 3 cups | (8 dl) | boiled potatoes, cubed, warm |
| 2 | (2) | hard boiled eggs, chopped, warm |
| 2 tbsp | (2 tbsp) | grated onion |
| 1 tbsp | (1 tbsp) | chopped green pepper |
| 2 tbsp | (2 tbsp) | chopped chives |
| | | salt and pepper to taste |
| ¾ cup | (2 dl) | French dressing (see page 134) |

Carefully mix together all ingredients except salad dressing which is poured on when everything is well blended. Cool. Just before serving, sprinkle with paprika, chopped parsley and chives. Serves 4.

# CRAB MEAT SALAD

| | | |
|---|---|---|
| 1 cup | (2½ dl) | cooked crabmeat, fresh or canned |
| ½ cup | (1 dl) | chopped celery |
| 2 tbsp | (2 tbsp) | mayonnaise |

Mix together all ingredients well and let mixture cool in refrigerator at least 1 hour before serving. Serve on crisp lettuce leaves or in the middle of a ring of a tomato aspic (see page 124). (Some aspic may be left over.) About 4 servings.

# TUNA SALAD

| | | |
|---|---|---|
| 1 can | (1 can) | tuna (about 7 oz or 2 hg) |
| ¾ cup | (2 dl) | chopped celery or chopped cucumber |
| 4 tbsp | (4 tbsp) | mayonnaise |

Break up tuna with a fork and mash. Add celery, mix well and add mayonnaise. Let mixture cool at least 1 hour in refrigerator before serving on crisp lettuce leaves or in sandwiches. If a stronger flavor is desired for this salad, 1 tbsp grated onion and 1 tbsp vinegar may be added. Serves 4–5.

# CURRIED TUNA SALAD

| | | |
|---|---|---|
| 1 can | (1 can) | tuna (about 7 oz or 2 hg) |
| ¼ cup | (½ dl) | mayonnaise |
| 1 tsp | (1 tsp) | curry powder |
| | | salt and pepper to taste |
| 2 | (2) | apples, peeled and cut into cubes |
| ½ cup | (1 dl) | cucumber, cut into small cubes |

Put tuna in a bowl and break apart with a fork. Mix spices with mayonnaise and add to tuna. Add apple and cucumber cubes and mix well. Cool at least 2 hours before serving on crisp lettuce leaves. Makes 4–5 portions.

Potato Salad, Liver Salad, Crab Meat Salad in Tomato Aspic Ring
with Deviled Eggs

## CHICKEN SALAD

*A classic summer salad, for picnics, cold suppers and similar meals.*

| | | |
|---|---|---|
| 2 cups | (5 dl) | cooked chicken, cut into cubes (recipe see page 93) |
| 1 cup | (2 dl) | chopped celery |
| 1 tbsp | (1 tbsp) | lemon juice |
| 4–5 tbsp | (4–5 tbsp) | mayonnaise |
| 2–3 | (2–3) | hard boiled eggs, cut in rather large pieces |
| | | salt and pepper to taste |

Mix together chicken, celery, lemon juice, mayonnaise, salt, pepper and blend well. Add eggs and mix carefully. Let salad cool for several hours. Makes 6 servings.

## MOCK CHICKEN SALAD

Proceed in same way as above but instead of chicken, use boiled or roasted veal, cut into cubes, or white tuna, with its oil rinsed away.

131

## CHICKEN SALAD ALOHA

| | | |
|---|---|---|
| 1½ cups | (4 dl) | boiling hot pineapple juice |
| 1 tsp | (1 tsp) | curry powder |
| 1½ cups | (4 dl) | Minute rice |
| ½ cup | (1 dl) | chopped dill pickles |
| 1 tsp | (1 tsp) | grated onion |
| | | pinch of pepper |
| 1½ cups | (4 dl) | cooked green peas |
| 1½ cups | (4 dl) | cooked chicken, cubed (recipe see page 93) |
| ½ cup | (1 dl) | chopped celery |
| ⅔ cup | (1½ dl) | mayonnaise |

Add curry to boiling pineapple juice in saucepan and mix in Minute rice. Cover and remove saucepan from heat, let stand about 10 minutes in order that the rice will soak up juice and spices. Stir rice with a fork to make it fluffy. Mix in remaining ingredients except mayonnaise and let mixture cool. Add mayonnaise and mix lightly with a fork. Garnish with lettuce leaves and tomato wedges. Makes 6 servings.


## LIVER SALAD

*An unusual way to serve liver, but both delicious and easily prepared.*

| | | |
|---|---|---|
| 1 lb | (½ kg) | beef or calves liver |
| 1 tbsp | (1 tbsp) | butter or margarine |
| 1 | (1) | medium onion, chopped (about ½ cup— 1 dl) |
| 2 | (2) | hard boiled eggs |
| | | salt and pepper to taste |
| 2 tbsp | (2 tbsp) | sherry |
| 2 tbsp | (2 tbsp) | mayonnaise |

Sauté onion in butter or margarine, brown liver slightly and simmer together with onion until tender. Grind in meat grinder together with hard boiled eggs. Add sherry, salt and pepper and mix well. Add mayonnaise. Form balls of mixture, sprinkle with chopped parsley and serve on crisp lettuce leaves. Garnish with tomato wedges and cucumber slices. Makes 5–6 servings.

## MACARONI TUNA SHRIMP SALAD

*An easily made salad that is a full meal in itself. Ideal to take with you for a day in the country—or to leave in the refrigerator for a quick supper when you return home.*

| | | |
|---|---|---|
| 1 cup | (2½ dl) | **elbow macaroni** |
| 2 | (2) | **hard boiled eggs, roughly chopped** |
| ¼ cup | (½ dl) | **chopped dill pickles or sweet pickles** |
| 4 tbsp | (4 tbsp) | **mayonnaise** |
| 1 | (1) | **medium tomato, cut into small pieces** |
| 1 | (1) | **can tuna** |
| ¼–½ lb | (1–2 hg) | **cooked shrimps (fresh or canned)** |

Boil macaroni in salted water about 10 minutes. Rinse well under running cold water so pieces will not stick together, and drain. Mix with hard boiled eggs, chopped pickles, tuna and shrimp. Put in refrigerator a few hours to cool. Mix in mayonnaise and tomato pieces, carefully. If desired, chopped fresh dill may also be added. Put on platter and garnish with crisp lettuce leaves, parsley and tomato wedges. Serves 4–5.

# FRENCH DRESSING

*Here are several recipes for salad dressings and good homemade mayonnaise, with different flavorings. But these are just a beginning. You can enjoy yourself experimenting with additional variations according to your own imagination. The possibilities are so many!*

| 1 cup | (2½ dl) | salad oil |
|-------|---------|-----------|
| ¼ cup | (½ dl) | vinegar |
| ¼ cup | (½ dl) | fresh lemon juice |
| 1 tsp | (1 tsp) | salt |
| 1 tsp | (1 tsp) | dry mustard |
| 1 tsp | (1 tsp) | paprika |

Put all ingredients in a bowl and beat vigorously until well blended. Pour into a glass jar or bottle and shake mixture each time it is to be used. Makes about 1½ cup (4 dl) dressing. Can be used as it is, or as a base for the following variations.

## SWEET FRENCH DRESSING
To ⅔ cup (1½ dl) French dressing as above add 2 tsp confectioners' sugar or honey. (If desired a little orange juice or pineapple juice may also be added).

## FRENCH DRESSING PIQUANT
To ⅔ cup (1½ dl) of French dressing as above, add 2 tbsp sugar and 1 tsp grated onion. Let a clove garlic stand in dressing for 1 hour, then remove.

## FRENCH DRESSING WITH ROQUEFORT CHEESE
Mix in ¼ cup (½ dl) Roquefort cheese (or other blue cheese), crumbled, and ½ tsp Worcestershire sauce to ⅔ cup (1½ dl) of French dressing as above.

## FRENCH DRESSING WITH CURRY
Add ½ tsp curry to ⅔ cup (1½ dl) French dressing as above.

## FRENCH DRESSING WITH KETCHUP
Add ⅔ cup (1½ dl) ketchup to ⅔ cup (1½ dl) French dressing as above.

# MAYONNAISE

| | | |
|---|---|---|
| 1 | (1) | egg yolk |
| 1 tsp | (1 tsp) | mustard |
| 1 tsp | (1 tsp) | confectioners' sugar |
| ¼ tsp | (¼ tsp) | salt |
| 1 tbsp | (1 tbsp) | fresh lemon juice or vinegar |
| 1 cup | (2½ dl) | salad oil |

Mix together all ingredients except oil and then beat vigorously while adding oil, first drop by drop, then evenly poured in larger quantities until mixture has thickened. If stronger flavor is desired, an additional 1 tbsp lemon juice or vinegar may be carefully added. Cool until mayonnaise is to be used. If desired, a little whipped cream may be added just before serving. Makes about 1½ cup (4 dl) mayonnaise.

# RUSSIAN DRESSING

| | | |
|---|---|---|
| ¼ cup | (½ dl) | ketchup |
| 1 tsp | (1 tsp) | chili sauce |
| 2 tbsp | (2 tbsp) | grated onion |

Add above ingredients to ½ cup (1¼ dl) mayonnaise as per previous recipe.

# THOUSAND ISLANDS DRESSING

| | | |
|---|---|---|
| 1 tbsp | (1 tbsp) | chili sauce |
| 1 tbsp | (1 tbsp) | chopped green olives |
| 1 tsp | (1 tsp) | chopped chives |
| 1 | (1) | hard boiled egg, chopped |
| ¼ tsp | (¼ tsp) | paprika |
| | | salt and pepper to taste |

Add the above ingredients to ⅔ cups (1½ dl) of mayonnaise as per above recipe. Mix well.

## SOUR CREAM MAYONNAISE

| | | |
|---|---|---|
| ¼ cup | (½ dl) | sour cream |
| 2 tsp | (2 tsp) | chopped chives |

Add the above ingredients to ¼ cup (½ dl) mayonnaise as per previous recipe.

## TARTAR SAUCE

| | | |
|---|---|---|
| 1 tsp | (1 tsp) | finely chopped green olives |
| 1 tbsp | (1 tbsp) | finely minced onion |
| 1 tsp | (1 tsp) | finely chopped dill pickles |

Add the above ingredients to ⅔ cup (1½ dl) mayonnaise as per previous recipe. Serve with fried fish.

## HORSE-RADISH CREAM DRESSING

| | | |
|---|---|---|
| ½ cup | (1 dl) | heavy cream |
| 1 tbsp | (1 tbsp) | vinegar |
| | | salt and pepper to taste |
| 2 tbsp | (2 tbsp) | grated horse-radish |
| 1 tsp | (1 tsp) | finely minced onion |

Whip cream until stiff, add vinegar little by little, beating constantly. Add the remaining ingredients and serve immediately.

# DESSERTS

Desserts are the opposite of salads so far as weight problems are concerned, and this is just as true in America as in other parts of the world. True, you can get by with fruit, either fresh or canned, but it is likely to taste better after you fix it up. To enjoy desserts, both in making them and eating them, it is best to just forget about calories for a while.

Pie is probably the most popular of all desserts in the United States, and it deserves to be. It is possible to fill a whole cookbook with just pie recipes, and still not include them all. I have just a small selection here, showing some of the best-liked kinds.

Chiffon pie filling is very similar to Swedish fromage and French cold soufflé puddings. You may make quite a variety of chiffon pies by using their recipes.

## INDIAN PUDDING

*A recipe for a dessert from olden times. Real corn meal of course gives the best result but you can make do with cream of wheat.*

| | | |
|---|---|---|
| ¼ cup | (½ dl) | corn meal (not Maizena!) or in lack of this, cream of wheat |
| 2 cups | (5 dl) | hot milk |
| ½ cup | (1 dl) | corn syrup |
| 1 | (1) | egg |
| 1 tbsp | (1 tbsp) | butter or margarine |
| 3 tbsp | (3 tbsp) | brown sugar |
| ½ tsp | (½ tsp) | salt |
| 1 tsp | (1 tsp) | cinnamon |
| ¼ tsp | (¼ tsp) | ginger |

Pour corn meal (or cream of wheat) in hot milk, stirring vigorously. Let simmer over very low heat for about 20 minutes and make sure it does not stick to bottom by stirring now and then. Remove from heat, add the remaining ingredients and mix well. Pour into a greased baking dish and bake uncovered in slow oven—325° F or 160° C—about 50 minutes. Serve pudding warm with cream or vanilla ice cream. 4–5 portions.

## PEACH MELBA

For each portion, cut a round piece of yellow or white cake. Put a scoop of ice cream on top and on top of this one half of a canned peach. Pour over 1–2 tbsp of the following Melba sauce and garnish with a little whipped cream, passed through a pastry tube if you want a fancy touch.

### Melba Sauce

| | | |
|---|---|---|
| 1 cup | (2½ dl) | fresh raspberries (or similar quantity of frozen ones) |
| ¼ cup | (½ dl) | currant jelly |
| ½ cup | (1 dl) | sugar |
| | | pinch of salt |
| ½ tbsp | (½ tbsp) | cornstarch (or potato starch) |
| 1 tbsp | (1 tbsp) | cold water |
| 1 tsp | (1 tsp) | fresh lemon juice |

Top: Pecan Pie, Boston Cream Pie
Bottom: Apple Pie, Lemon Chiffon Pie

Pass raspberries through a sieve to remove pits. Mix together currant jelly, sugar and sieved raspberries in a small saucepan and bring to a boil. Add a pinch of salt, cornstarch mixed with water and lemon juice and stir vigorously until mixture has been brought to a boil again and the sauce is transparent. Strain sauce and chill well before serving.

## AMBROSIA

*A light dessert, easy to make and to eat. It is especially appreciated after a heavy meal.*

| | | |
|---|---|---|
| 1 cup | (2 dl) | heavy cream |
| 1 cup | (2 dl) | crushed pineapple, fresh cooked or canned |
| ½ cup | (1 dl) | shredded coconut |

Whip cream until stiff and mix in crushed pineapple, well drained, and coconut. Serve immediately in dessert bowls. For 5-6.

## JELLIED RHUBARB MOLD

*A good, refreshing dessert that is a change from rhubarb stew and soup.*

| | | |
|---|---|---|
| 1 lb | (½ kg) | tender young rhubarb stalks |
| | | a few drops of red food coloring |
| 1 cup | (2½ dl) | sugar |
| ½ cup | (1 dl) | water |
| 1 tbsp | (1 tbsp) | gelatin powder |

**For garnish:**

| | | |
|---|---|---|
| ½ cup | (1 dl) | heavy cream, whipped |
| | | grated peel of half an orange |

Wash rhubarb, cut into small pieces and boil them over low heat together with sugar and water until soft, but not so long that they fall apart. Drain the hot juice into gelatin powder which first has been softened in ¼ cup (½ dl) cold water. Stir until gelatin is dissolved, add coloring, then pour in rhubarb. Pour into a mold and cool in refrigerator at least 3 hours. Unmold gelatin and serve with whipped cream, somewhat sweetened, and flavored with grated orange peel. Makes 4–6 servings.


## COFFEE JELLY WITH CUSTARD SAUCE

*Make this one especially for coffee hounds and people who do not like sweet desserts.*

| 1 cup | (2 dl) | sugar |
| 3 tbsp | (3 tbsp) | gelatin powder |
| 3 cups | (8 dl) | strong, hot coffee |
| 1 tbsp | (1 tbsp) | fresh lemon juice |

Mix together sugar and gelatin powder in a heavy saucepan. Add hot coffee and 1½ cup (3½ dl) water. Bring to a boil, stirring constantly and simmer until sugar is completely melted. Remove from heat and add lemon juice. Pour into a mold and let cool in refrigerator 5–6 hours, or over night. Unmold carefully and serve with custard sauce. For 6–8 portions.


**Custard Sauce:**

| 1 | (1) | egg |
| 1½ cups | (4 dl) | milk |
| 2 tbsp | (2 tbsp) | sugar |
| 1 tsp | | vanilla extract *or* |
| | (1 tbsp) | vanilla sugar |
| ½ tbsp | (½ tbsp) | potato starch (or cornstarch) |

Mix together all ingredients except vanilla in a heavy saucepan. Let sauce simmer over low heat, stirring constantly until somewhat thickened. Remove from heat and continue beating until cold, then add vanilla. If desired ¼–½ cup (½–1 dl) heavy cream may be added.

# APPLE CRISP

*Desserts with apples in different combinations have top popularity in the United States, and in many other countries also. This one is easily prepared and delicious, and may be called either pudding or cake.*

| | | |
|---|---|---|
| 6 | (6) | medium tart, juicy apples, peeled and cut into pieces |
| ½ cup | (1 dl) | sugar |
| 1 cup | (2 dl) | water |
| 1 tsp | (1 tsp) | cinnamon |

Mix together all ingredients and boil 10 minutes, then pour into a greased baking dish. On top put a mixture prepared with the following:

| | | |
|---|---|---|
| ½ cup | (1¼ dl) | brown sugar |
| 6 tbsp | (6 tbsp) | butter or margarine |
| 1 cup | (2½ dl) | flour |
| 1½ tsp | (1½ tsp) | baking powder |

Mix together flour, baking powder and brown sugar, then cut in butter or margarine with two knives or pastry cutter until mixture is crumbly. Sprinkle over apples in baking dish and bake in medium oven—350° F or 175° C—40 minutes. Serve pudding warm with whipped cream, vanilla ice cream or vanilla custard sauce. Makes 5-6 servings.

## APPLE BROWN BETTY

| | | |
|---|---|---|
| 1½ cups | (4 dl) | cornflakes, crushed until crumbly |
| 1 tsp | (1 tsp) | nutmeg |
| 2 tbsp | (2 tbsp) | butter or margarine, room temperature |
| ⅓ cup | (¾ dl) | brown sugar |
| 4 cups | (1 l) | sliced apples (about 6–8 tart apples) |
| 1 tsp | (1 tsp) | cinnamon |
| 2 tsp | (2 tsp) | grated lemon peel |

Mix together cornflakes crumbs, nutmeg and butter. Put apples in a large bowl and mix together with brown sugar, cinnamon, and grated lemon peel. Put half of apple mixture in a greased baking dish and pour half of cornflakes mixture over it. Add remaining apple mixture and on top of this remaining cornflakes mixture. Bake with cover on dish (aluminum foil will do) in medium-warm oven—375° F or 190° C—30 minutes. Remove cover and bake an additional 15 minutes or until apples are tender. Pudding is best served warm, plain or with custard sauce, vanilla ice cream or cream. About 6 portions.

## PINEAPPLE-APPLE CRISP

| | | |
|---|---|---|
| 4 cups | (1 l) | thinly sliced tart apples (about 1 kg) |
| 1 can | (1 can) | pineapple, cut-up 1½–2 cups (4–5 dl) |
| 1 tbsp | (1 tbsp) | fresh or canned lemon juice |
| 1 cup | (2 dl) | brown sugar |
| ¼ cup | (60 g) | butter or margarine, melted |
| 1 tsp | (1 tsp) | cinnamon |
| | | pinch of salt |
| 1½ cups | (4 dl) | cornflakes, crushed |

Make alternate layers of apple slices and pineapple pieces in a greased baking dish. Sprinkle with lemon juice. Mix together remaining ingredients and put on top. Cover baking dish (aluminum foil will do) and bake 30 minutes in medium oven—350° F or 175° C—remove cover and bake an additional 25 minutes or until apples are completely tender. Serve pudding warm with whipped cream, custard sauce or vanilla ice cream. For 6.

## FRUIT COCKTAIL CRISP

| | | |
|---|---|---|
| 1 cup | (2½ dl) | brown sugar |
| 1 | (1) | egg |
| 1 cup | (2 dl) | flour |
| ½ tsp | (½ tsp) | salt |
| 1 tsp | (1 tsp) | baking soda |
| 1 can | (1 can) | fruit cocktail, 1½–2 cups (4–5 dl) |
| 1 tsp | | vanilla extract *or* |
| | (1 tbsp) | vanilla sugar |
| ½ cup | (1¼ dl) | brown sugar mixed with ⅔ cup (1½ dl) chopped nuts |

Mix together 1 cup (2½ dl) brown sugar, egg, flour, salt and baking soda and blend well. Add fruit cocktail (well drained) and vanilla. Pour into a greased and floured baking dish. Mix together ½ cup (1¼ dl) brown sugar and nuts or almonds and sprinkle on top. Bake in medium oven—350° F or 175° C—about 30 minutes or until cake is nicely golden in color. Serve warm with whipped cream, light cream or vanilla sauce. Serves 5-6.

## APPLE PIE

*Pie is without doubt number one of all American desserts. And among the pies, apple is the favorite. It is excellent just plain (hot or cold) or with a piece of cheddar cheese beside it. But people who do not count calories are likely to pile vanilla ice cream on top, for pie à la mode.*

Apple Pie

Select firm, tart and juicy apples. 2 lbs (1 kg) apples usually correspond to 6 medium apples or 6 cups (1½ l) sliced apples, which is about the right amount for an American apple pie.

| | | |
|---|---|---|
| 1 | (1) | double pie crust (see page 43) |
| 6 cups | (1½ l) | sliced apples |
| ¾–1 cup | (1¾–2½ dl) | sugar depending on tartness of apples |
| 1 tbsp | (1 tbsp) | flour |
| 1 tsp | (1 tsp) | cinnamon |
| | | pinch of nutmeg |
| | | juice of ½ lemon |
| 1½ tbsp | (1½ tbsp) | butter or margarine |

Mix together sugar, flour and spices, and mix with apples. (If apples are of a very juicy variety, sprinkle an additional 1 tbsp. flour on the bottom of pie crust). Pile apples in crust, mounding up in center. Sprinkle lemon juice on top, dot with butter and cover with upper crust. Cut out small vents in cover, to let steam escape during baking. Make a nice fluted edge with fingers, or with a fork, around pie crust as per illustration on page 42. Bake in hot oven—425° F or 220° C—50-60 minutes. The pie may be served either warm or cold, plain, or with light cream, whipped cream, or ice cream. Serves 6–8.

## FRENCH APPLE PIE

| | | |
|---|---|---|
| 1 | (1) | single pie crust (see page 41) |

For filling use the same ingredients as the previous recipe but with minimum quantity of sugar. Instead of covering with pie crust, make a special topping with the following ingredients:

| | | |
|---|---|---|
| ½ cup | (110 g) | butter or margarine |
| ½ cup | (1¼ dl) | brown sugar |
| 1 cup | (2½ dl) | flour |

Mix flour and sugar. Add butter and cut with two knives or pastry blender until mixture is crumbly and crumbs are of the size of a pea. Put this mixture on top of filling and bake in medium-hot oven—400° F or 200° C—45–55 minutes. Serve warm with cream or vanilla ice cream.

## DUTCH APPLE PIE

Follow recipe for Apple Pie but make the vents on top crust a little larger. Five minutes before pie is done, take out of oven and pour ½ cup (1 dl) heavy cream through vents. Put pie back and bake until ready.

## STRAWBERRY AND RHUBARB PIE

| 1¼ cups | (3 dl) | sugar |
|---|---|---|
| ½ cup | (1 dl) | flour |
| 1 cup | (2½ dl) | fresh strawberries (or 1 10-oz pkg frozen) |
| 2 cups | (5 dl) | rhubarb, cut into small pieces |
| 2 tbsp | (2 tbsp) | butter or margarine |
| 1 | (1) | double pie crust (see page 43) |

Sift together flour and sugar and mix ¾ of this with berries and rhubarb. Roll out half of pie crust and put into a pie plate, scatter remaining ¼ flour and sugar mixture on it then add filling and dot with butter. Roll out remaining dough and cut strips of dough and put in a criss-cross design on top. Bake in hot oven—425° F or 220° C—for 10 minutes. Turn down heat to 350° F or 175° C and bake an additional 30 minutes, or until rhubarb is completely tender.

# BLUEBERRY PIE

*This is probably a good second in popularity among pies. In America, blueberries are considered truly American, but in North Europe I am sure they are thought of as truly European.*

| | | |
|---|---|---|
| 4 cups | (1 l) | blueberries |
| 1½ tbsp | (1½ tbsp) | fresh lemon juice |
| 1 tbsp | (1 tbsp) | grated lemon peel |
| ¾ cup | (1¾ dl) | sugar |
| ¼ tsp | (¼ tsp) | salt |
| 2 tbsp | (2 tbsp) | flour, or 1½ tbsp tapioca |
| 1 | (1) | double pie crust (see page 43) |

Rinse and clean blueberries and drain. Put into a bowl and add lemon juice, lemon peel, sugar, salt and flour (or tapioca). Put fruit into pie crust, dampen edges and cover with more crust. With fingers or a fork, pinch together edges to make sure they are closed. Cut some vents in top crust to let steam escape during baking. Bake in hot oven—450° F or 240° C—for 10 minutes, then turn down heat to medium—350° F or 175° C—and bake an additional 30 minutes. The pie may be served either warm or cold; with or without whipped cream or vanilla ice cream.

# FRESH PLUM PIE

| | | |
|---|---|---|
| 3 cups | (¾ l) | fresh plums (pits removed) |
| 1¼ cups | (3 dl) | sugar |
| 2 tbsp | (2 tbsp) | flour |
| 2 tbsp | (2 tbsp) | fresh lemon juice |
| | | pinch of salt |
| 1 tbsp | (1 tbsp) | butter |
| 1 | (1) | double pie crust (see page 43) |

Mix together plums, sugar, flour, lemon juice and salt. Put mixture in a pie crust and dot with butter. Cover with more pie crust and cut a few vents in top to let steam escape during baking. Bake in very hot oven—425° F or 220° C—10 minutes, turn down heat to medium—350° F or 175° C—and bake an additional 35 minutes or until plums are completely tender. Serve warm or cold with whipped cream or vanilla ice cream.

## BANANA CREAM PIE

| 1 cup | (2 dl) | sugar |
|---|---|---|
| ½ cup | (1 dl) | flour |
| 1 tsp | (1 tsp) | salt |
| 2 cups | (5 dl) | milk |
| 2 | (2) | egg yolks, slightly beaten |
| 1 tsp | | vanilla extract *or* |
| | (1 tbsp) | vanilla sugar |
| 3 | (3) | large, well-ripened bananas |
| 1 | (1) | single, pie crust, baked (see page 41) |

Heat milk, but do not let it boil. Mix sugar, flour and salt in a heavy saucepan, pour in the hot milk, a little at a time stirring vigorously until mixture is smooth. Bring to a boil, turn down heat and let simmer until it thickens. Mix a little of the pudding with the slightly beaten egg yolks, then return it to saucepan and add vanilla. Let simmer for a little while, but do not let it boil, as the mixture would then curdle. Remove from heat, let cool for a few minutes. Slice bananas evenly over bottom of the baked pie crust (set aside ½–¾ of a banana to use for decoration), pour pudding on top and cool. Just before serving, decorate with remaining banana slices. If desired, a meringue may be spread over top in the same manner as for Lemon Meringue pie (see page 152), or it may be decorated with whipped cream.

## BUTTERSCOTCH PIE WITH BANANAS

| | | |
|---|---|---|
| ¾ cup | (1¾ dl) | brown sugar |
| 5 tbsp | (5 tbsp) | flour |
| ½ tsp | (½ tsp) | salt |
| 2 cups | (5 dl) | milk |
| 2 | (2) | egg yolks, slightly beaten |
| 2 tbsp | (2 tbsp) | butter |
| 1 tsp | | vanilla extract *or* |
| | (1 tbsp) | vanilla sugar |
| 3 | (3) | well-ripened bananas, sliced |
| 1 | (1) | single pie crust, baked (see page 41) |

Mix together sugar, flour and salt and stir in milk, a little at a time, in a heavy saucepan (or double boiler) and let it simmer until mixture has thickened, stirring constantly. Cover and simmer an additional 10 minutes over low heat, stirring off and on. Add a little of this mixture to slightly beaten egg yolks, then pour back into sauce pan and simmer for another minute while stirring, but it must not boil, as mixture may curdle. Add butter and vanilla and cool somewhat. Pour mixture in a baked pie crust in layers alternately with sliced bananas, and if desired, garnish with whipped cream.

## COCONUT CUSTARD PIE

*A very good—but ah, how rich—dessert.*

| | | |
|---|---|---|
| 2 | (2) | eggs |
| ½ cup | (1 dl) | sugar |
| | | pinch of salt |
| | | pinch of nutmeg |
| 1¼ cups | (3 dl) | hot milk |
| 1 tsp | | vanilla extract *or* |
| | (1 tbsp) | vanilla sugar |
| 1 cup | (2 dl) | shredded coconut |
| 1 | (1) | unbaked single pie crust (see page 41) |

Beat eggs slightly and add remaining ingredients, mixing well.

Pour mixture in the unbaked pie crust and make sure edges of pie crust do not fold over and let filling run out during baking. Bake in hot oven—450° F or 220° C—15 minutes, turn down heat to medium—350° F or 175° C—and bake an additional 10–15 minutes. The pie is cooked when a knife stuck into it about 1″ (3 cm) from the edge comes out dry. The middle of pie may seem a little thin, but it will get firm after standing for a while.

## OLD FASHIONED EGG PIE

| | | |
|---|---|---|
| 1 cup | (2 dl) | sugar |
| 2 tbsp | (2 tbsp) | flour |
| 2 | (2) | eggs |
| ½ cup | (110 g) | butter or margarine, melted |
| ¼ cup | (½ dl) | buttermilk or sour milk |
| 1 | (1) | unbaked single pie crust (see page 41) |

Mix together sugar and flour, beat eggs slightly and add and continue beating until mixture is thick and fluffy. Add butter and buttermilk (sour milk) and pour mixture into pie crust. Bake in medium-hot oven—375° F or 190° C—40–50 minutes. Pie is best when served warm, but it may also be eaten cold.

# PECAN PIE

*This delicacy originated in the South where pecan trees are plentiful.*
*It is rich and sweet, but mmmmm how good!*

| 2 | (2) | eggs |
|---|---|---|
| ½ cup | (1¼ dl) | sugar |
| ½ tsp | (½ tsp) | salt |
| ¼ cup | (½ dl) | melted butter |
| ¾ cup | (1¾ dl) | dark corn syrup |
| ½ cup | (1¼ dl) | pecans (halves, not chopped) |
| 1 | (1) | unbaked single pie crust (see page 41) |

Mix together eggs, sugar, salt, butter and syrup and beat until mixture is thick and fluffy. Mix in pecans and pour mixture into unbaked pie crust, or place pecans on top. Bake in medium-hot oven—375° F or 190° C—40–50 minutes, or until pie is firm and nicely golden brown. Serve warm or cold. If desired, pecans may be replaced by walnut halves.

# OATMEAL PIE

*This pie, although based on plain old oatmeal, has much of the taste quality of pecan pie at lower cost. It is exceptionally easy to make.*

| 2 | (2) | eggs, slightly beaten |
|---|---|---|
| ¾ cup | (1¾ dl) | sugar |
| ¾ cup | (1¾ dl) | light corn syrup |
| ¾ cup | (1¾ dl) | quick-cooking oatmeal |
| ¾ cup | (1¾ dl) | shredded coconut |
| ½ cup | (110 g) | butter or margarine |
| 1 | (1) | unbaked single pie crust (see page 41) |

Mix together eggs, sugar and syrup and beat until mixture is thick and fluffy. Add oatmeal, coconut and butter and mix well. Pour mixture into unbaked pie crust and bake in hot oven—375° F or 190° C—45 minutes.

Top: Cucumber Mold, page 122

Bottom: Pecan Pie

# SHOO FLY PIE

*I have tried to find the origin of this name, but have not been able to. This pie is a soft spice cake in a pie crust, and comes from the Pennsylvania Dutch people. They are descendants of Germans who settled parts of the state hundreds of years ago, and they have stubbornly held to many of their good old ways in cooking and in many other skills.*

| | | |
|---|---|---|
| ¾ cup | (2 dl) | flour, sifted |
| ½ cup | (1¼ dl) | brown sugar |
| | | pinch of salt |
| ¼ cup | (30 g) | butter, margarine or other shortening |
| ½ tsp | (½ tsp) | baking soda |
| ¼ cup | (½ dl) | boiling water |
| ¼ cup | (½ dl) | molasses |
| 1 | (1) | single pie crust, unbaked (see page 41) |

Mix together flour, sugar and salt and cut in butter or margarine with two knives or pastry blender until mixture is crumbly. Put baking soda into the boiling water and add molasses. Add this liquid to ¾ of flour mixture and blend well. Pour batter into an unbaked pie crust, pour remaining flour mixture on top and bake in hot oven—450° F or 225° C—10 minutes, then turn down heat to 350° F or 175° C and bake an additional 20–30 minutes, or until pie is firm. The pie may be served either warm or cold, plain or with whipped cream.

Cookout, including hamburgers, page 73

# GRASSHOPPER PIE or
# CREME DE MENTHE PIE

*This festive dessert is so rich that you should serve it in small pieces. It must be cold, and is extra good when frozen.*

**Crust:**

| | | |
|---|---|---|
| 18 | (18) | chocolate cookies, crushed |
| 6 tbsp | (100 g) | butter or margarine |

**Filling:**

| | | |
|---|---|---|
| 28 | (28) | large marshmallows |
| ½ cup | (1¼ dl) | milk |
| ¼ cup | (½ dl) | creme de menthe |
| 1 cup | (2 dl) | heavy cream |

Crush chocolate cookies (they should be a dark kind with strong chocolate flavor). Melt butter and mix chocolate crumbs with it, then press mixture into a pie pan and bake in medium oven—350° F or 175° C—about 5 minutes.

Mix marshmallows with milk in a heavy saucepan or double boiler over low heat and simmer until marshmallows have melted. Let mixture cool and add liqueur and place in refrigerator until thoroughly cool. Whip cream, stir into marshmallow mixture and pour into cooled pie crust. Sprinkle with some cookie crumbs on top and let cool at least 5 hours before serving. Or it may be placed in freezer for a few hours and then served completely frozen, or partly thawed.

# LEMON MERINGUE PIE

*Another dessert that is typically American. It is handsome and delicious, and gives a final touch of elegance to a good meal. It is a little complicated to make, but well worth the trouble.*

| | | |
|---|---|---|
| 1¼ cups | (3 dl) | sugar |
| 4 tbsp | (4 tbsp) | corn starch (or potato starch) |
| 1¼ cups | (3 dl) | water |
| 2 | (2) | egg yolks |

| | | |
|---|---|---|
| 2 tbsp | (2 tbsp) | butter |
| 3 tbsp | (3 tbsp) | fresh lemon juice |
| 1 tbsp | (1 tbsp) | grated lemon peel |
| 1 | (1) | single pie crust, baked (see page 41) |
| For Meringue: | | |
| 2 | (2) | egg whites |
| | | pinch of cream of tartar, if desired |
| 3 tbsp | (3 tbsp) | sugar |

Mix together sugar, starch and water in a heavy saucepan and bring to a boil, stirring constantly. Boil for one minute, then pour about half of mixture over slightly beaten egg yolks, stir, then pour it all back into saucepan. Simmer for an additional minute or so, but do not let it boil because of danger of curdling. Mix in remaining ingredients and blend well, then pour mixture into baked pie crust. Spread meringue mixture immediately over the hot pudding and bake in hot oven—400° F or 200° C—8–10 minutes. Put pie on a rack in a rather warm room out of draft and serve as soon as it has cooled.

**Meringue:** Beat egg whites together with cream of tartar (if such is used) until stiff. Add sugar, a little at a time, and continue beating until sugar has dissolved. Make sure that the meringue is spread all the way out to the edges of the pie crust, otherwise it will easily shrink towards the middle, when it is being baked.


## LEMON CHIFFON PIE

*Chiffon pies are very much like the Swedish fromage-desserts or the French cold soufflés, except that they have the distinction of being served in pie crust, which we think improves both taste and appearance. There are many varieties, of which only a few are given here.*

| | | |
|---|---|---|
| 1 cup | (2½ dl) | sugar |
| 1 tbsp | (1 tbsp) | gelatin powder |
| ¾ cup | (1¾ dl) | water |
| ⅓ cup | (¾ dl) | fresh lemon juice |
| 4 | (4) | eggs |
| 1 tbsp | (1 tbsp) | grated lemon peel |
| 1 | (1) | baked single pie crust (see page 41) |

Mix together ½ cup (1¼ dl) sugar, gelatin powder, water, lemon juice and 4 egg yolks in a heavy saucepan and simmer over low heat until thickened. Stir constantly, but make sure mixture does not boil, as it would then curdle. Stir in grated lemon peel, put saucepan in cold water and cool until mixture has thickened. Fold in a meringue which has been made by beating the egg whites and the remaining sugar until stiff. Blend well and pour mixture into a baked pie crust and cool pie for several hours until completely firm. Serve with whipped cream, if desired.

## PUMPKIN CHIFFON PIE

| | | |
|---|---|---|
| 3 | (3) | eggs |
| ⅔ cup | (1½ dl) | brown sugar |
| 1½ cups | (4 dl) | cooked or canned pumpkin |
| ½ cup | (1¼ dl) | milk |
| ½ tsp | (½ tsp) | salt |
| 1 tsp | (1 tsp) | cinnamon |
| ½ tsp | (½ tsp) | nutmeg |
| 1 tbsp | (1 tbsp) | gelatin powder |
| ¼ cup | (½ dl) | cold water |
| ½ cup | (1 dl) | sugar |
| 1 | (1) | baked single pie crust (see page 41) |

Put egg yolks, brown sugar, pumpkin, milk and spices in a heavy saucepan or double boiler and let simmer until mixture has thickened somewhat. Dissolve gelatin powder in cold water and add to pumpkin mixture, stirring well, then let it cool. Beat egg

whites until stiff, adding ½ cup (1 dl) sugar, a little at a time. Carefully fold meringue into pumpkin mixture and pour it into a baked pie crust. Cool in refrigerator for a couple of hours before serving. Serve plain or with whipped cream.

## MOCHA CHIFFON PIE

*For coffee lovers this should be THE pie!*

| 1 tbsp | (1 tbsp) | gelatin powder |
|---|---|---|
| ¼ cup | (½ dl) | cold water |
| ⅓ cup | (¾ dl) | cocoa |
| 1 cup, scant | (2 dl) | sugar |
| | | pinch of salt |
| 3 | (3) | eggs |
| 1 tsp | | vanilla extract *or* |
| | (1 tbsp) | vanilla sugar |
| 1 cup, scant | (2 dl) | strong coffee |
| 1 | (1) | baked single pie crust (see page 41) |

Soften gelatin in cold water. Mix together cocoa, half of sugar, salt and add slightly beaten egg yolks mixed with the coffee. Let simmer in a heavy saucepan, or double boiler, until mixture has thickened but make sure it does not boil, as it might then curdle. Put saucepan in cold water to cool and when mixture is rather firm in consistency, add egg whites (which first have been beaten with remaining sugar to make a stiff meringue) and vanilla. Mix carefully and pour into baked pie crust. Cool pie for several hours before serving. Top with whipped cream, if desired.

# COCOA CREAM ROLL

| | | |
|---|---|---|
| 3 | (3) | eggs |
| 3 tbsp | (3 tbsp) | flour |
| 2½ tsp | (2½ tsp) | baking powder |
| | | pinch of salt |
| ⅔ cup | (1½ dl) | confectioners' sugar |
| 2½ tbsp | (2½ tbsp) | cocoa |

**For filling and decoration:**

| | | |
|---|---|---|
| 1 cup | (2 dl) | heavy cream |
| | | a little dark chocolate |

Separate eggs and beat egg whites until stiff. In a separate bowl beat yolks until thickened and mix them carefully with whites. Carefully add mixed dry ingredients and stir until blended. Spread batter in a large baking dish, about 8 x 12" (20 x 30 cm) on a slightly oiled brown paper. Bake in medium hot oven—375° F or 190° C—about 15 minutes. Remove cake from pan and put it on a slightly damp towel, which is sprinkled with sugar. Carefully pull off paper and cut away dry edges if such have formed during baking, and roll the cake together while still warm. Roll the damp towel around cake and allow it to cool. Unroll and spread with whipped cream, roll it together again, spread whipped cream on top and sides and sprinkle flaked chocolate on top.

# BOSTON CREAM PIE

*The following dessert, which is called "pie" in the United States, has really nothing to do with pies as such. But it is a good—although rich—cake, which is welcome as a dessert and at the coffee or tea table.*

| | | |
|---|---|---|
| 2 | (2) | eggs |
| 1 cup | (2½ dl) | sugar |
| ½ tsp | (½ tsp) | salt |
| 1 tsp | | vanilla extract, *or* |
| | (1 tbsp) | vanilla sugar |

| | | |
|---|---|---|
| 1 tbsp | (1 tbsp) | butter or margarine |
| ⅔ cup | (1½ dl) | hot milk |
| 2 tsp | (2 tsp) | baking powder |
| 1¼ cups | (3 dl) | flour |

Beat eggs and sugar until white and fluffy, add salt and vanilla. Bring milk to a boil, add butter or margarine and when melted, add to egg mixture. Add flour, sifted together with baking powder, and mix well. Pour into a greased baking pan and bake in medium oven—350° F or 175° C—25-30 minutes. Let cake cool and cut it into two layers. Put one layer on a serving dish and spread with a vanilla custard cream made as follows:

| | | |
|---|---|---|
| ¼ cup | (½ dl) | sugar |
| 1 tbsp | (1 tbsp) | corn starch (or potato starch) |
| 1 cup, scant | (2 dl) | milk |
| 1 | (1) | egg yolk, slightly beaten |
| 1 tbsp | (1 tbsp) | butter |
| 1 tsp | | vanilla extract *or* |
| | (1 tbsp) | vanilla sugar |

Mix together sugar, corn starch and milk in a small heavy saucepan and bring to a boil, beating constantly. Remove from heat and continue beating vigorously for a few seconds, then add slightly beaten egg yolk. Add butter and vanilla and mix well. Let mixture cool, stirring now and then. When filling is completely cool, spread on bottom cake layer and put top layer carefully on top. Then pour or spread the upper surface with the following icing:

| | | |
|---|---|---|
| 3 tbsp | (3 tbsp) | cocoa |
| 3 tbsp | (3 tbsp) | butter or margarine |
| 1 cup | (2½ dl) | confectioners' sugar |
| 4 tbsp | (4 tbsp) | boiling water |

Melt butter or margarine in a small heavy saucepan over very low heat, add cocoa and mix well, then add sifted confectioners' sugar and the boiling water. Mix only until icing is evenly blended. Spread this icing carefully over cake and let it drip by itself over the edges.

# RUM CAKE

| | | |
|---|---|---|
| 2 | (2) | eggs |
| ⅔ cup | (1½ dl) | sugar |
| 2 tbsp | (2 tbsp) | melted butter |
| ⅓ cup | (¾ dl) | light cream |
| 1½ cups | (3½ dl) | flour |
| 2 tsp | (2 tsp) | baking powder |

For decoration:

| | | |
|---|---|---|
| ½ cup | (1 dl) | heavy cream |
| | | almonds or walnuts |

Beat eggs and sugar until white and fluffy, add butter and light cream alternately with flour, which first has been sifted together with baking powder. Pour batter preferably in a ring baking dish and bake cake in medium oven—350° F or 175° C—35-40 minutes. After cake has been removed from oven, let it stand for a few minutes, and then carefully loosen around the edges and bottom to make sure it will not stick to pan. Then pour the following mixture on top:

| | | |
|---|---|---|
| ½ cup | (1 dl) | sugar |
| ½ cup | (1 dl) | water |
| ¼ cup | (½ dl) | rum (or a little more, if desired) |

Bring all the ingredients to a boil and then pour over cake immediately. Put cake in a cold place and let it stand for several hours. Just before serving, take it out of baking pan and spread with whipped cream and garnish with chopped walnuts or almonds.

# COFFEE RUM TORTONI

| | | |
|---|---|---|
| 2 tbsp | (2 tbsp) | finely chopped almonds |
| 1 cup | (2½ dl) | heavy cream |
| ½ cup | (1¼ dl) | confectioners' sugar |
| 2 tsp | (2 tsp) | instant coffee |
| 2 tbsp | (2 tbsp) | rum |
| 1 | (1) | egg white |

Sprinkle finely chopped almonds on a baking plate and put into a hot oven—400° F or 200° C for a few minutes until nicely golden in color, then remove and put aside. Whip cream until thick and mix in confectioners' sugar little by little. Mix together instant coffee with rum in a cup and add carefully to whipped cream. Beat egg white until stiff, and carefully fold into cream mixture. Put mixture into small paper containers (for cup cakes), sprinkle chopped almonds on top and put into freezing compartment of refrigerator or freezer and keep them there until completely frozen. Makes 6-8 containers.

## BAKED ALASKA

*A tricky and pleasing dessert. It is really not difficult to make, and it has a nice surprise effect when you serve meringue right out of a hot oven, and the guests find that it is filled with ice cream.*

| 1 | (1) | cake layer |
|---|---|---|
| 1 qt | (1 l) | ice cream |
| 3 | (3) | egg whites |
| ⅔ cup | (1½ dl) | sugar |

Place cake layer on a large serving platter, cover with ice cream and put in freezing compartment until just before serving. Make a meringue of egg whites and sugar, beating until stiff, and cover ice cream and cake with a thick layer of this, making sure that all parts of the ice cream are completely covered by meringue. Put it in a very hot oven—475° F or 240° C—for 2-3 minutes, or only until the meringue gets a golden color. Serve immediately. Makes 6-8 servings.

## CREAMY CHOCOLATE FREEZE

| 2 | (2) | eggs |
|---|---|---|
| 1 cup | (2 dl) | cream or evaporated milk |
| ½ cup | (1 dl) | sugar |
| ½ cup | (1 dl) | chocolate syrup (see page 167) |

Beat eggs until thick and fluffy. Mix in remaining ingredients and pour mixture into ice tray and freeze until firm. Remove mixture from ice tray, break it into pieces and beat again until smooth. Pour the mixture back into the ice tray and freeze again 2–3 hours before serving.

## GLAZED CHEESE CAKE

Use recipe for Graham Cracker Crust, page 43, but double the quantity of sugar. Pat mixture into a 10″ (25 cm) pie pan or low baking dish.

**For filling:**

| 1 lb | (about ½ kg) | cream cheese, room temperature |
|---|---|---|
| ¾ cup | (1¾ dl) | sugar |
| 1 tsp | | vanilla extract *or* |
| | (2 tsp) | vanilla sugar |
| 3 | (3) | eggs |

Blend cream cheese and sugar, add vanilla and eggs and continue stirring until mixture is smooth. Pour into shell and bake in 325° F or 160° C oven for 30–35 minutes or until firm. Cool before adding glaze.

**Glaze:**

| 2 cups | (5 dl) | frozen sliced strawberries, defrosted |
|---|---|---|
| 3 tbsp | (3 tbsp) | cornstarch |
| 2 tbsp | (2 tbsp) | lemon juice |

Drain strawberry juice into saucepan, add starch and stir until smooth. Bring to a boil and cook for one minute or until thick and clear. Remove from heat and add lemon juice. Carefully fold in berries. Cool glaze and spread on top of cheese cake and chill in refrigerator until serving.

# MISCELLANEOUS

This last chapter has an assortment of recipes that would not fit properly under any of the earlier headings. It is ironical that it should bring to you at the end of the book what is first served in the morning—the American pancake—and also the appetizers and dips that are served before dinner.

## FAVORITE PANCAKES

*As you will find from the recipes, the American pancakes are quite different from those in other countries. They are served hot off the griddle for breakfast, with maple syrup. If maple is not available, you can make a good substitute by following the recipe on page 167.*

| 1 | (1) | egg |
|---|---|---|
| 1¼ cups | (3 dl) | buttermilk or sour milk |
| 2 tbsp | (2 tbsp) | butter or margarine, melted |
| 1¼ cups | (3 dl) | flour, sifted |
| 1 tbsp | (1 tbsp) | sugar |
| 1 tsp | (1 tsp) | baking powder |
| ½ tsp | (½ tsp) | baking soda |
| ½ tsp | (½ tsp) | salt |

Beat egg, milk and melted butter until well blended, then mix in the dry ingredients. Continue beating until thick and fluffy. Drop by tablespoonfuls about 3–4 at a time, on a hot griddle or frying pan, which has first been brushed with butter. Cook until golden brown on both sides and serve piping hot with maple syrup, pancake syrup (see page 167) or fruit sauce and a dab of butter on each pancake.

## BLUEBERRY PANCAKES

Add 1 cup (2 dl) fresh or frozen blueberries to the above recipe just before cooking. Otherwise proceed in the same manner.

## BANANA PANCAKES

Add 2 bananas, sliced thinly, to recipe just before cooking.

# OATMEAL PANCAKES

| 1½ cups | (4 dl) | oatmeal |
| 2 cups | (5 dl) | buttermilk (or sour milk) |
| ½ cup | (1¼ dl) | flour |
| 1 tbsp | (1 tbsp) | sugar |
| 1 tsp | (1 tsp) | baking soda |
| 1 tsp | (1 tsp) | salt |
| 2 | (2) | eggs, slightly beaten |

Mix together buttermilk and oatmeal. Add the remaining ingredients and blend well. Drop by tablespoonfuls on a hot griddle or frying pan which has first been brushed with melted butter. Make 3–4 at a time, depending on the size of the griddle. Serve piping hot with fruit sauce or maple syrup and a dab of butter on each pancake.

# WESTERN OMELET

*This omelet is a favorite one in practically all diners and coffee shops. For convenience, proportions for one egg are given here. For an omelet, you can mix and cook it this way, or as many batches together as you wish. For a sandwich, the one-egg mixture is just right.*

**For each portion use:**

| 1 | (1) | egg |
| 1 tbsp | (1 tbsp) | milk or cream |
| 1 tbsp | (1 tbsp) | finely chopped ham |
| 1 tbsp | (1 tbsp) | finely chopped onion |
| 1 tbsp | (1 tbsp) | finely chopped green pepper |
| | | salt and pepper to taste |
| 1 tbsp | (1 tbsp) | butter or margarine |

Sauté onion and green pepper in butter for a few minutes in an omelet pan or small frying pan, then add ham. Pour in egg which has first been slightly beaten together with milk, and cook omelet until set. May be served just plain, with several batches cooked together, but it is most popular in individual servings in sandwiches. Remember, the American sandwich consists of two slices of bread with a filling in between.

# PIZZA PIE

*This specialty, originally from Italy, has made itself an important place in American eating. Here, it is made with tomato sauce or tomato concentrate, rather than with the fresh tomatoes used in many countries.*

| | | |
|---|---|---|
| 1 tsp | (1 tsp) | dry yeast |
| 1 cup, scant | (2 dl) | lukewarm water |
| 2–2½ cups | (6–7 dl) | flour |

Dissolve yeast in lukewarm water and add flour, a little at a time, then knead dough until it is elastic. Let rise in a warm place until double in bulk. Roll out dough into two large, thin cakes (about 12" (35 cm) in diameter) and roll up outer edges somewhat to make an edge. This makes two pies.

**Sauce:**

| | | |
|---|---|---|
| 2 cans | (2 cans) | tomato paste (about 1 cup—2 dl) |
| 1 tsp | (1 tsp) | oregano |
| | | salt and pepper to taste |

Mix together spices and tomato paste and spread over pizza dough. Sprinkle with

| | | |
|---|---|---|
| ¼ cup | (½ dl) | grated Parmesan cheese |
| 1½ cups | (4 dl) | roughly grated Mozzarella cheese |

Bake in hot oven—425° F or 220° C—20–25 minutes.

Other items may also be added on top of the pizza pie before baking, such as

| | | |
|---|---|---|
| 5–6 | (5–6) | chopped anchovies fillets |
| ⅔ cup | (1½ dl) | fresh or canned mushrooms |
| | | mashed meatballs |
| | | thin-sliced sausage |

It is also possible to make small individual pizza pies from English Muffins (see page 10). Instead of baking them in the oven, you put the filling and cheese on the baked and split muffins and put them in the oven under the broiler until cheese is melted.

# BREAD AND BUTTER PICKLES

*Most American housewives no longer go to the trouble of making their own pickles. But here is a good recipe from a few years ago, which usually produces better pickles than you are likely to find in a store.*

| | | |
|---|---|---|
| 1 gallon | (4 l) | fresh cucumbers |
| 8 | (8) | small onions |
| 2 | (2) | green peppers |
| ⅔ cup | (1½ dl) | salt |

Wash cucumbers and cut into paper-thin slices. Cut onions and peppers in very thin slices also. Mix salt with cucumbers, onion and peppers in a large crock or dish, pour in about 1 qt (1 l) of crushed ice, put a cover directly on top of cucumbers with a weight on it and let stand for three hours. Drain all liquid. Put mixture into a large kettle and add the following ingredients:

| | | |
|---|---|---|
| 5 cups | (1¼ dl) | sugar |
| 2 tsp | (2 tsp) | tumeric |
| 1 tsp | (1 tsp) | ground cloves |
| 3 tsp | (3 tsp) | mustard seeds |
| 1 tsp | (1 tsp) | celery seeds |
| 5 cups | (1¼ dl) | vinegar |

Place kettle over low heat and stir now and then with a wooden spoon. Heat to scalding point but do not boil. Pour immediately into hot, sterilized glass jars and seal. The pickles may be eaten after about a week but flavor improves during longer storing.

# WHITE SAUCE

*I am quite sure that everyone who reads this cookbook knows how to make a plain white sauce. But since it is used in a number of these recipes, it is safest to give you an American version of it.*

| | | |
|---|---|---|
| 2 tbsp | (2 tbsp) | butter or margarine |
| 2 tbsp | (2 tbsp) | flour |
| 1½–2 cups | (4–5 dl) | milk |
| | | salt and pepper to taste |

Melt butter or margarine in a saucepan, add flour and mix well, add milk, a little at a time, stirring vigorously until sauce is thick and smooth. Add salt and pepper to taste.

## CHEESE SAUCE

Add ½–⅔ cup (1–1½ dl) grated cheese, (Cheddar type is good) to the above white sauce and simmer over low heat, stirring constantly, until cheese is completely melted.

## COCKTAIL SAUCE

*This sauce is used when serving tidbits such as shrimp or crabmeat as appetizers.*

| 2 cups | (5 dl) | tomato ketchup |
|---|---|---|
| 1 tbsp | (1 tbsp) | grated horse-radish |
| 1 tbsp | (1 tbsp) | vinegar |
| 1½ tsp | (1½ tsp) | Worcestershire sauce |
| | | a few drops of tabasco |
| | | salt and paprika to taste |

Mix together all ingredients in a small heavy saucepan and let simmer for about 20 minutes. Let sauce get completely cool before using.

## BARBECUE SAUCE

*This sauce is used both for marinating the meat before cooking, and brushing on it while it is grilling or broiling. It gives the meat a special flavor.*

| 1 tbsp | (1 tbsp) | butter or margarine |
|---|---|---|
| ⅓ cup | (¾ dl) | finely minced onion |
| 2 tsp | (2 tsp) | brown sugar |
| 2 tbsp | (2 tbsp) | vinegar |
| 1 tbsp | (1 tbsp) | dry mustard |
| 2 tsp | (2 tsp) | Worcestershire sauce |

| ¼ tsp | (¼ tsp) | salt |
|-------|---------|------|
| 1 cup | (2½ dl) | tomato ketchup |
| 1 cup | (2½ dl) | warm water |
| 1 tbsp | (1 tbsp) | fresh lemon juice |

Melt butter or margarine in a saucepan and sauté onion about 10 minutes. Add all the remaining ingredients, except lemon juice. Let simmer over low heat and stir now and then until mixture has thickened. Then add lemon juice. This sauce is suitable for meat, smoked meat and frankfurters. Makes about 2 cups (5 dl) barbecue sauce.

## CHOCOLATE SYRUP

| 1 cup | (2½ dl) | cocoa |
|-------|---------|-------|
| 1½ cups | (4 dl) | sugar |
| ½ cup | (1¼ dl) | corn syrup |
| ¼ tsp | (¼ tsp) | salt |
| 1½ tsp | (1½ tsp) | vinegar |
| 1 tsp | | vanilla extract *or* |
| | (1 tbsp) | vanilla sugar |

Mix together all ingredients except vanilla in a small saucepan and bring to a boil, then let simmer over low heat for about 5 minutes, stirring constantly. Remove from heat and add vanilla. Cool mixture and pour into glass jars which must be kept refrigerated if sauce is to be kept for some time.

This type of sauce is very popular in U.S. and is suitable to serve on top of vanilla ice cream and different puddings. It may also be used in frostings for cakes. It is most popular for "chocolate milk" for the children, which can be made by adding 1–2 tsp. of syrup to a glass of milk and mixing well.

## HOMEMADE PANCAKE SYRUP

| 1 cup | (2½ dl) | sugar |
|-------|---------|-------|
| 1 cup | (2½ dl) | brown sugar (dark or light) |
| 1 cup | (2½ dl) | water |

Mix together all ingredients in a saucepan and bring to a boil. Simmer over low heat until all sugar is melted and a thin syrupy consistency has been obtained. If maple flavoring is available, it may be added.

## ONION DIP

*It is customary in most of the United States to serve cocktails before dinner, at least when there are guests. The cocktails are generally accompanied by something light and crisp to eat, such as chips, crackers, cheese or nuts. The chips and crackers are made more interesting by providing a thick sauce or dip in which they can be dipped just before eating. Almost anything goes in making up a dip, and you can just let your imagination roam. Here are examples of some of the more common types.*

| | | |
|---|---|---|
| 1 tbsp | (1 tbsp) | butter |
| 1 | (1) | large onion, finely minced |
| 2 tbsp | (2 tbsp) | water |
| 1 | (1) | bouillon cube |
| 1 cup | (2 dl) | sour cream |
| 1 tsp | (1 tsp) | grated horse-radish |
| 1 tbsp | (1 tbsp) | ketchup |

Brown butter in frying pan and add onion, sautéing until golden brown, add water and bouillon cube and simmer for about 5 minutes. Put onion mixture in a bowl and add remaining ingredients. Refrigerate for several hours before serving with potato chips or something similar.

## SOUR CREAM ANCHOVY DIP

| | | |
|---|---|---|
| 1 cup | (2 dl) | sour cream |
| 3 tbsp | (3 tbsp) | mayonnaise |
| 5–6 | (5–6) | anchovy fillets, finely chopped |
| ¼ cup | (½ dl) | finely chopped chives |

Mix together all ingredients in a bowl and let mixture chill for several hours before serving with potato chips or something similar.

## TUNA ROQUEFORT DIP

| | | |
|---|---|---|
| 1 can | (1 can) | tuna |
| ¼ lb | (1 hg) | roquefort cheese (or other blue cheese) |
| 1 cup | (2 dl) | sour cream |
| 1 tsp | (1 tsp) | fresh lemon juice |

Drain tuna well and mash contents in a bowl. Add cheese, which has first been crumbled up, then sour cream and lemon juice. Beat vigorously until mixture is smooth and chill for several hours before dip is served with potato chips or something similar.

## SWISS CHEESE DIP

| | | |
|---|---|---|
| ½ cup | (1 dl) | grated Swiss cheese |
| 1 cup | (2 dl) | mayonnaise |
| ¼ cup | (½ dl) | heavy cream |
| | | salt and pepper to taste |

Whip cream and mix with remaining ingredients. Chill and serve with potato chips, salty crackers or ham cubes.

## CRABMEAT DIP

| | | |
|---|---|---|
| 1 cup | (2 dl) | mayonnaise |
| 1 can | (1 can) | crabmeat (about 1 cup–2 dl) |
| ¼ cup | (½ dl) | finely chopped green pepper |
| ¼ cup | (½ dl) | tomato, finely chopped |
| | | pepper to taste |
| 1 tsp | (1 tsp) | fresh lemon juice |

Mix together all ingredients and chill. Serve with potato chips or salty crackers.

## CREAMY PINK DIP

| | | |
|---|---|---|
| ½ cup | (1 dl) | mayonnaise |
| ¼ cup | (½ dl) | sour cream |
| ¼ cup | (½ dl) | ketchup |

Mix together all ingredients and chill. Serve with cooked shrimp.

## ORIENTAL DIP

| | | |
|---|---|---|
| 1 cup | (2 dl) | mayonnaise |
| 2 tbsp | (2 tbsp) | minced chives |
| 2 tbsp | (2 tbsp) | milk |
| 1 tsp | (1 tsp) | ginger |
| 1 tsp | (1 tsp) | vinegar |
| 4 tsp | (4 tsp) | soy sauce |

Mix all ingredients well and chill. Serve with raw vegetables, such as green pepper cut into long strips, cucumbers cut into strips, carrots cut into strips, cauliflower cut into bite size pieces, radishes etc.

# GORGEOUS GLOP

*This recipe is only a cheese paste which is a good spread for crackers and chips that are served as appetizers.*

| | | |
|---|---|---|
| 3 tbsp | (3 tbsp) | salad oil |
| 2 | (2) | cloves garlic, crushed |
| 1 tbsp | (1 tbsp) | caraway seeds |
| 1 tbsp | (1 tbsp) | oregano |
| 2 cans | (2 cans) | tomato soup (condensed) |
| ½ lb | (¼ kg) | cheese of Cheddar type, roughly grated or chopped |

Brown garlic in oil and add the next three ingredients. Bring to a boil, then add grated or chopped cheese. Simmer slowly until cheese is completely melted, stirring constantly. Add pepper, salt, ground cloves and cinnamon to taste. Beat mixture until smooth and pour into small containers and refrigerate. Suitable as a spread for cocktail crackers etc. Mixture will keep for a long time if containers are covered (with plastic or foil) so that mixture does not dry out during storing.

# CHOPPED CHICKEN LIVERS

| | | |
|---|---|---|
| ½ lb | (2 hg) | chicken livers |
| 1 | (1) | small onion, finely chopped |
| 1 tbsp | (1 tbsp) | butter or margarine |
| 1 | (1) | hard boiled egg, chopped |
| 1 tbsp | (1 tbsp) | sherry |
| | | salt and pepper to taste |
| 1 tbsp | (1 tbsp) | mayonnaise |

Sauté onion in butter or margarine, add chicken livers and simmer over low heat about 10 minutes. Grind liver, onion, and egg in a meat grinder, or chop it up finely with a fork. The mixture should be somewhat crumbly. Stir with sherry, salt, pepper and 1 tbsp. mayonnaise. Serve on crackers as a cocktail snack, or put on a leaf of lettuce, decorate with a tomato wedge and slice of cucumber and serve as appetizer.

# INDEX

# APPENDIX

## AMERICAN AND METRIC MEASURES

### VOLUME

|  | Teaspoon (tsp) | Tablespoon (tbsp) | Fluid ounce (fl. oz.) | Cup | Deciliter (dl) |
|---|---|---|---|---|---|
| Teaspoon | 1 | $\frac{1}{3}$ | $\frac{1}{6}$ | $\frac{1}{64}$ | .05 |
| Tablespoon | 3 | 1 | $\frac{1}{2}$ | $\frac{1}{16}$ | .15 |
| Fluid ounce | 6 | 2 | 1 | $\frac{1}{8}$ | .30 |
| Cup | 48 | 16 | 8 | 1 | 2.37 |
| Deciliter | 20.3 | 6.76 | 3.38 | .42 | 1.00 |

1 pint = 2 cups      1 quart = 2 pints      1 liter = 10 deciliters

### WEIGHT

1 kilogram = 1000 grams          1 kilogram = 2.20 pounds
1 hectogram = 100 grams          1 hectogram = 3.52 ounces
1 pound = 16 ounces              1 gram = .035 ounce
1 pound = .45 kilogram           1 ounce = 28.35 grams

# TEMPERATURE CONVERSION

Farenheit and Celsius (Centigrade) temperatures may be converted into each other by use of either of the following formulas:

$$\text{Temperature, Farenheit} = \frac{9 \times \text{Temperature, Celsius}}{5} + 32$$

$$\text{Temperature, Celsius} = \frac{5 \times (\text{Temperature, Farenheit} - 32)}{9}$$

This conversion works out to whole numbers every 5 degrees on the Celsius scale and every 9 degrees on the Farenheit scale, as in the table below, where equivalent temperatures on the two scales are placed beside each other.

| Faren-heit | Celsius | Faren-heit | Celsius | Faren-heit | Celsius |
|---|---|---|---|---|---|
| **−40** | **−40** | 149 | 65 | 329 | 165 |
| −31 | −35 | **150** | **65.5** | 338 | 170 |
| −22 | −30 | 158 | 70 | 347 | 175 |
| −13 | −25 | 167 | 75 | **350** | **176.6** |
| − 4 | −20 | 176 | 80 | 356 | 180 |
| **0** | **−17.7** | 185 | 85 | 365 | 185 |
| 5 | −15 | 194 | 90 | 374 | 190 |
| 14 | −10 | **200** | **93.3** | 383 | 195 |
| 23 | − 5 | 203 | 95 | **392** | **200** |
| **32** | **0** | **212** | **100** | **400** | **204.4** |
| 41 | 5 | 221 | 105 | 401 | 205 |
| 50 | 10 | 230 | 110 | 410 | 210 |
| 59 | 15 | 239 | 115 | 419 | 215 |
| 68 | 20 | 248 | 120 | 428 | 220 |
| **72** | **22.2** | **250** | **121.1** | 437 | 225 |
| 77 | 25 | 257 | 125 | 446 | 230 |
| 86 | 30 | 266 | 130 | **450** | **231.1** |
| 95 | 35 | 275 | 135 | 455 | 235 |
| **100** | **37.7** | 284 | 140 | 464 | 240 |
| 104 | 40 | 293 | 145 | 473 | 245 |
| 113 | 45 | **300** | **148.9** | **482** | **250** |
| **122** | **50** | **302** | **150** | 491 | 255 |
| 131 | 55 | 311 | 155 | **500** | **260** |
| 140 | 60 | 320 | 160 | 600 | 315.5 |